Forward

This book was a long time coming. I want to begin by thanking Kimble Knowlden, my former boss and mentor, for helping me set this goal. Years ago, as part of a team building exercise, Kimble asked us to set down a long-term goal, something completely unrelated to our jobs, a "wish list", if you will. Mine was pretty easy for me. Having always loved cooking and entertaining, it was my dream to write a cook book with stories about the meals and people we shared them with. Well, I did it! I'm sure Kimble doesn't even remember giving out that assignment, but there it is just the same. It goes to show you that you never can underestimate the power of the words you choose to say and how they will be received. Kimble and his wife, Susy are a class act. I am lucky to know them both.

To my husband, Louis, you know you are never second on my list. Where would I ever be without you? There is so much that I can say, but you already know that. This book is for you, plain and simple.

To my daughter, Antoinette and her family, thank you. You give me so much joy, you have no idea!

Finally, to my friends and family who provided the inspiration for the recipes and stories in this book, I hope you enjoy it and understand the love I have for all of you.

Dedication

I dedicate this book to the 343 members of the FDNY who gave their lives on September 11, 2001. Please take time to remember them, and all the other victims who perished on that awful day.

With that said, we have the responsibility to carry on our American traditions and live up to the values we hold so dear. Enjoy time with your families, teach them your traditions, respect your histories, pass on what you have learned.

Table of Contents

The Circle of Life	Page 4
Section I - the Family	Page 6
Baked Stuffed Artichokes	Page 8
Marinara Sauce	Page 11
Pasta Carbonera	Page 14
Swiss Roll-Up Meatloaf	Page 16
Bacon Cheeseburger Meatloaf	Page 18
Dijon Garlic Leg of Lamb	Page 19
Mom's Vinegar Chicken	Page 20
Christmas Eve Anchovy Bread	Page 21
Mashed Potato Pie	Page 23
Beet and Onion Salad	Page 24
Beet Salad with Greens	Page 25
Aunt Ida's Ricotta Cake	Page 26
Aunt Rose's Pumpkin Bread	Page 27
Donna's Beauty Shoppe Carrot Cake	Page 29
Photos for this Section	Pages 31 - 39
The Greek Connection	Page 40
Pan Fried Halloumi Cheese	Page 42
Greek Meatballs (Keftedes)	Page 44
Stuffed Grape Leaves 2 ways	Page 46
Moussaka (Eggplant Casserole)	Page 48
Galatoboureka (Custard Pie)	Page 50
Ravanie Cake	Page 52
Photos for this Section	Pages 54 - 63
Section II - Firehouse Memories	Page 64
Tasmanian Chicken	Page 65
Firehouse Meatloaf	Page 67
Ribs on the Run	Page 69
Fire Starter Peppers	Page 71
Red Tide Pot Roast	Page 73
Photos for this Section	Pages 76 - 77
Section III - Friends	Page 78
Pizza Rustica	Page 80
Cheese Straws	Page 82
Antoinette's Birthday Chicken Meatloaf	Page 83
Mango Coulis	Page 84
Linda's Baked Chicken with Salsa	Page 85
Terry's Puerto Rican Style Beans	Page 87
Baked Fish in a Pouch	Page 89

Table of Contents

Papaya Salsa	Page 90
Stir Fried Tofu and Watercress	Page 92
Summer and Spring Rolls	Page 93
Rugelach Cookies	Page 95
Neopolitan Honey Balls	Page 97
Photos for the Section	Pages 99 - 102
Author's Note and Photos	Page 103

The Circle of Life - Growing up Family Style in The Bronx
A Collection of Favorite Recipes and Stories

By Victoria Kikis

A family packs up their car and heads off for Thanksgiving dinner. Christmas mornings are met with the cozy aroma of fresh baked cinnamon rolls. Easter week begins with the ritual of coloring dozens of hard boiled eggs. Summer barbecues fill the air with pungent charcoal and heavenly spices. Your favorite birthday cake is that yellow cake with chocolate icing that always tastes so good. No restaurant lasagna could ever compare to the one from your mom's kitchen. There's your favorite Christmas cookie, always tasting as delicious as you remember, year after year. Traditions baked with love and care fresh from the oven. From the largest houses to the simplest bungalows, somehow we all seem to gather together in the kitchen.

We may travel the world, see all manner of sights and sounds. We arrive home and empty our suitcases of new memories and blend them with old familiar ones. The circle of life comes back to the simple pleasures of hearth and home.

In this book I try to share the wonderful times I've been lucky to experience over the years. Every recipe carries with it a touch of love, a memory of good times and good company. As you read through it, think about where you come from. Remember the warmth of family times. Bring them back into your life. Share them with those you love. Pass it on; the circle widens and welcomes us all.

SECTION I
The Family — Life as we loved it!

Family was the center of our lives when I was growing up. Today there is such a disintegration of the core family that I am so thankful for the great years I had. Oh, make no mistake, there were lots of crazy times, but in the end, the glue that held us all together, making us ever stronger, was our family ties.

My dad, Louis Testa, and my mom, Mary De Guilio Testa, were both WWII veterans. After the war, mom and dad settled in a quaint little house in the Fordham section of The Bronx, New York. It was a kind of a bungalow on Valentine Avenue, off of the Grand Concourse. It had a big yard and all the neighborhood kids would come over to our house to play. All around us there were mostly apartment buildings We loved our little patch of green. Things started getting more crowded and, shortly after my dad became a member of the New York City Police Department, he looked for even greener pastures and moved us across the borough to Throgg's Neck. We moved into one of the first group of row houses to be built in that section, all the way at the end of East Tremont Avenue, just a half block from the East River. What a great place to grow up! I was just 5 years old then. We had plenty of vacant "lots" to explore. There were swamps with shallow ponds that froze over in the winter, providing us with some fun and very precarious ice skating. Our block, and the whole neighborhood, really, was made up of mostly City workers, Police and Firefighters, Sanitation workers, and the odd small business owner or two. We were Italian, Irish, and German for the most part.

My mom's family all lived way upstate in the Rochester/Buffalo area. We saw them only from time to time. My dad, on the other hand, had his family almost all in the same borough as us! Grandpa Joseph lived on Radcliff Avenue. His 4 sisters all lived close too. Aunt Fran lived next door to Grandpa, Aunt Bette lived in the Burke Avenue projects, (both in my dad's precinct). Aunt Rose lived a bit away on the Grand Concourse and Auntie Anne lived in Woodlawn. Sundays were family gathering days and we often all met at our house for endless Sunday dinners. It didn't matter how large or small your house was. We never though about it! We always had fun, squeezing in and sharing wonderful meals together. We never really rushed through things then. I remember taking breaks between courses and walking with my grandpa down to Fort Schuyler, talking about nothing in particular, just enjoying the fresh air.

Dad loved having people around. He loved fooling around with recipes and trying out new things. One of the first things he did when we got to our new house was to build a brick barbecue in our tiny backyard. What fun he had with that! His most famous invention was the stuffed hamburger. He took it a step further and made the stuffed meatloaf roll. My cousin Johnny still talks about those hamburgers today. That grill stood the test of time, and is still standing today, almost 60 years later.

It was a very special thing, growing up in the 'neighborhood." Storekeepers all knew you. My dad, and most of the other families, all had accounts with the local grocery (S&W). When mom needed something, she thought nothing of sending us the 3 blocks up to the store and picking up the eggs, or milk, or bread we needed. No money involved. We just asked the owners, Pat or Ben, to "put it on the bill." Every payday my dad would pay the tab and all was well with the word. I must confess to stopping in a few times to buy bags of chips or a soda even though my mom didn't send me! My dad never said a word!

I am really happy to say that today, Throgg's Neck is still a thriving neighborhood. Oh, it is way busier than ever. While you might find a grocer willing to "put it on the bill," that time has long past. Yet, you can still find great mom and pop stores, awesome pizza joints, really good restaurants, and enjoy a little taste of the seaside from the nearby waterfront. There are still long-time families living there, and, you can be pretty sure that if you walked around the block for the newspaper, you'd bump into a neighbor or two on the way.

Some things coming out of that neighborhood and making their way into these pages are memories and recipes from old favorite restaurants, families and friends. Enjoy!

Recipes in this section:

Baked Stuffed Artichokes
Marinara Sauce
Pasta Carbonera
Dad's Swiss Roll Mashed Potato Meat Loaf
Bacon Cheeseburger Meat Loaf
Dijon Garlic Roast Leg of Lamb
Mom's Sunday Vinegar Chicken
Christmas Eve Anchovy Bread
Mashed Potato Pie
Beet and Onion Salad
Beet Salad with Greens
Aunt Ida's Ricotta Cake
Aunt Rose's Pumpkin Bread
Donna's Beauty Shoppe Carrot Cake
    The Greek Connection —
Pan Fried Halloumi
Greek Meatballs - Keftedes
Stuffed Grape Leaves (Dolmades) 2 ways
Moussaka
Ravanie (farina) Cake
Galatoboureka (phyllo-custard pie)

BAKED STUFFED ARTICHOKES

The Artichoke King

My dad just loved artichokes. Lots of households never even saw an artichoke but we always had some around the house. Whether canned artichoke hearts for the salad, or marinated hearts in our antipasto, my dad couldn't get enough. It was really fun to see how much he enjoyed them. Those who knew my dad know how much he enjoyed all foods, but artichokes were by far his all time favorite. He used to call them "ArDEEchokes" in his true Bronx accent.

We all loved them. They were a special part of our holiday and "company" dinner tables. I always remember my grandfather coming over and getting together with my mom and dad in the kitchen to prepare, what in our minds, was the most grandest of artichoke dishes: baked stuffed artichokes. It was a process and everyone put his or her two cents in as to the best way to trim the chokes. What knife to use, to pre-boil or not, how to keep them from turning color. And then, of course there was the stuffing. What were the best fillings? My grandpa liked to add pignolli (pine) nuts and raisins. Mom and dad liked capers. Sometimes we even added anchovies. Everything was worth a taste test and we were all happy to take part.

When my cousin, Walter Jachens Jr. (Skipper), invited us out to his wedding, my husband and I convinced my mom and dad to make the trip too. Skip lived in the San Francisco area and dad's sister, Fran, was mother to the groom. It would be my parent's first trip to the west coast and we told them about all the great things they would be seeing. The day after the wedding we made a road trip down the Pacific Coast Highway and up the inland rout through the massive farmlands. We drove the famous 17-Mile Drive down through the Del Monte Forest and visited the quaint town of Carmel. Forget all that..dad would nod here and there at one scenic view after another UNTIL we came to the town of Castroville! Then his eyes lit up. We were in the Artichoke Capital of the World!! He was in his glory. We stopped at a local restaurant and took photos next to a gigantic artichoke. We had lunch made up of artichokes, artichokes, and more artichokes. It was a trip he remembered for the rest of his life The seals and otters playing in the waves of the Pacific Ocean had nothing on the venerable artichoke as far as my dad was concerned.

It is believed that artichokes have special properties that help digestion, lower cholesterol and other healthy benefits. I don't think my dad ever cared about any of that. I do know that he loved them and we remember him every time we have them. The dish itself is very simple…just a few ingredients. Good olive oil is a must. Don't be put off by the preparation process. Make it fun; believe me the end result is truly worth it.

And now the recipe - Baked Stuffed Artichokes

4 large fresh artichokes
1 cup Italian flavored breadcrumbs
1 teaspoon salt
1 tablespoon capers, chopped
2 tablespoons fresh shopped Italian parsley
1/4 cup grated parmesan cheese
1 tablespoon lemon juice for the artichoke water and 1 tablespoon for the cooking water
1/4 cup (approx) olive oil

1. Prepare artichokes. Rinse whole artichokes and pat dry. Remove outer leaves. These are too tough to eat. Cut stem off at base, being careful not to cut into the bottom. This is for stability. Cut off the top of each vegetable (you want to have all the pointed ends cut leaving you with a kind of vegetable bowl.). Gently part the inner leaves until you expose the fibrous "choke" at the bottom core. Use a teaspoon and begin pulling out the small yellow/purplish leaves and the choke hairs. Once this is done, place the artichoke in a bowl of cold water with lemon juice so that it will not turn color. Continue cleaning the remaining vegetables. When you have all the artichokes cleaned, keep them in the water. Now take the stems you cut off earlier. Peel each one and set aside in the cold lemon water.
2. Prepare for stove top by selecting a pot that will hold your artichokes snuggly. You don't want them tipping over. I use crunched up aluminum foil on the bottom as a support.
3. Sit the vegetables face-up in the pot and add about 1/2 cup water to the bottom. Add the stems. You need just enough water so that the stems float. Add lemon juice. Simmer on medium heat for about 15 minutes.
4. While the stems are simmering, mix the stuffing. In a bowl combine breadcrumbs, capers, parsley, cheese, salt and pepper. Add 1/2 the olive oil. Mix well and set aside.
5. Preheat oven to 375.
6. Remove artichokes and stems from the pot. Take the stems and chop them finely. Add these to your stuffing mixture. Add more oil a bit at a time to get the stuffing to the right consistency. You don't want it too oily. Crumbly and moist is what you are aiming for.
7. Spoon mixture into each artichoke, packing firmly.
8. Place artichokes in an oven-proof baking dish, securing them in place if needed as before with foil.
9. Place a small amount of water in bottom and cover securely. Bake in oven for 20 minutes. Raise heat to 475 and heat uncovered 5 minutes more or until tops are browned.

Serve the artichokes as an appetizer with sliced lemon. You can make them the star of a light dinner by adding a salad and some crusty bread. Artichokes are hard to pair with wines. Try a sparkling water with lemon wedge and enjoy.

Hint: You can enjoy these beautiful vegetables simply steamed by following recipe steps 1 through 3. They are great served at room temperature or nice and hot with fresh lemon or a light garlic mayonnaise.

MARINARA SAUCE

One of the best things I can recommend to anyone is to make your own marinara sauce. Is it a very simple process and, once you have made your own, you'll wonder why you waited so long to try it.

It's The Sauce!

When I was growing up, Sundays were special days. Most stores were closed back them; it was a time for family and friends - not hustle and bustle. In our neighborhood, Sundays began with church or Sunday School. After church we would walk home, stopping off at the bakeries for buns and rolls, and a loaf of Italian bread for the Sunday meal. We got the "buns" (sweet rolls like cheese filled Danish, spicy cinnamon crumb) at the German bakery, and the rolls and bread at the Italian one. It was long agreed by all that for cakes, the Germans did better than the Italians! On the other hand, you really couldn't beat the fresh breads and cannolis Primrose Bakery turned out. Discussions about these fine points were part of conversations between us kids and adults alike. It was a wonderful dilemma to be faced with.

Once we got the baked goods, the next stop was to pick up the newspaper at Mrs. Victor's Stationery, and then walk the 3 blocks home. That was a challenge! How to make it home without resisting the urge to tear off the top of the Italian bread and pop it in your mouth for a savory snack before reaching your front door.

Equally tantalizing on these trips was the aroma wafting from the houses as you passed. It was a pretty sure bet that 4 out of 5 families we knew would be sitting down to a Sunday dinner of pasta and some meat simmered long and low in a bubbling red tomato sauce. Every mom had her own style. Some called it gravy, some called it sauce. Some kept it pure; some loaded it up with beef and pork. No matter, all was well with the world when there was the smell of tomato, garlic and herbs in the air!

We all ate wonderful family-style mid-afternoon meals in those days. Some started as early as 2pm, some as late as 5, with most families sitting down at 3pm. During those hours the streets would turn quiet with the gentle accompaniment of the sounds of clinking glasses and silverware to plate. We talked and ate, laughed, cleared the table, stored the leftovers. It was all part of the fabric of the day.

After the meal, doorbells would start ringing as we kids began "calling" for each other to come out. The kids would go out to play, the parents would settle down for cards or TV. In summer we would stay out until dark, playing hide and seek, hanging out on frot porches (stoops), walking to the nearby candy store. Winters were shortened by early sunsets and school the next day. We'd watch TV; maybe have a snack of those leftovers and then to bed.

The comfort foods we love come from those exciting tastes and smells and are best enjoyed tempered gently with memories of the times and people we care for.

The Recipe: Marinara Sauce

2 28 oz cans tomatoes (whole or crushed)
2 cloves garlic (chopped)
1/4 cup fresh Italian parsley (chopped)
4 fresh basil leaves (chopped)
2 dry bay leaves
1 medium onion (chopped)
2 -3 tablespoons olive (more or less to your taste)
1 teaspoon each salt and pepper

1. Prepare your tomatoes by opening each can. If you are using whole tomatoes, get a small bowl and empty the juice from the can into the bowl. Taking another larger bowl, empty the tomatoes into that. Using your hands, gently crush the tomatoes. Add the juice to the tomatoes.
2. In a 3 quart saucepan add the olive oil. Set the heat to medium and add in the bay leaves.
3. Add the onion and stir, then after about a minute, add in the garlic. Be careful not to burn the garlic or it will taste bitter. Stir the mixture and, once the garlic is blended with the onions, add the rest of your fresh, chopped herbs.
4. Now you are ready to add your tomatoes. Be mindful that they will splatter quickly. Add the tomatoes about half at a time, stirring to keep the sauce from bubbling. Add the salt and pepper. You can adjust your seasonings as the sauce simmers.
5. Bring the sauce to a boil then cover, and reduce heat to low.
6. Simmer on low heat for about 1/2 hour.

This sauce gets better with time. After the 1/2 hour, taste to see if you want to add more salt or pepper. You can serve it right away or let it sit. I usually make my sauce in the morning and let it stand, covered throughout the day, until dinner time.

Whole or crushed tomatoes? It is really a matter of personal taste. I like to use whole because I can rush the tomatoes to the consistency I like. We like a rustic sauce with chunks of tomato. The crushed tomatoes are often packed in paste and you get a thicker consistency than with the whole ones. If you find it too thick, you can thin it out by adding a bit of wine or water. Bringing the sauce up to a boil, turning off the heat and covering it tightly will also add steaming liquid to the sauce. Try that first, you may not need to add anything else.

Easy Variations: A good red sauce goes a long way. This basic recipe can be used to make several delicious dishes. The simple marinara becomes a robust puttanesca by just chopping up about 1/4 cup calamata olives, 1 tablespoon capers and a can of flat anchovy fillets. Add a little olive oil to the bottom of a pan and sauté the ingredients. Add 2 cups of marinara sauce and a bit of chopped, fresh parsley. Cover and simmer for about 15 minutes. Done!

How about the classic linguini with red clam sauce? Add a little olive oil to the saucepan and heat. Now add 1 bottle of clam juice and 1 can chopped clams (with their juices) to the pan. Add 1 cup of marinara sauce. Cover and simmer for about 10 minutes. Done! Want it spicy? Add a teaspoon of crushed red pepper flakes.

For the meat lovers, just take about 1 pound of ground beef, turkey, or chicken and sauté in your saucepan. Now either add 2 cups of pre-made marinara and simmer, or, if you are making it fresh, pick up the recipe from step 2.

Pasta Carbonera with Rosemary

Growing up in The Bronx in the 50's and 60's was a blast. My parents moved us to a section called Throgg's Neck back in 1955 when I wash just 4 years old. Our home was among the first series of attached brick, affordable housing for blue-collar families just starting out. Our "block" was made up of Italian, Irish and German families. The dads were mostly police, fire and sanitation men, and a few moms (like mine) worked outside the home. Eating out was a real treat for us.

We basically had 4 restaurants to choose from in those days. 3 were Italian and one was Chinese. Of the Italian, 2 were casual, family-style restaurants (Tom's and *Louis Seafood). The third was a very stylish, more upscale one called Amerigo's. We almost always went to Tom's or the Chinese. Once in a great while we got to go to Amerigo's. The decor was pure "Rat Pack," black marble walls, red velvet banquettes. A lush waterfall cascaded over the entire back wall of the dining room. The lighting and service were subtle with a capital **S**. A place meant to linger in. It was also a favorite place for our local "wise guys." As a kid it was always exciting and a bit scary to eat there but the food was always wonderful.

My husband, Louis, moved to our neighborhood in his early teens. He wasn't all that familiar with Amerigo's or Italian food other that lasagna or pizza. HIs parents immigrated to the United States from Cyprus. They were a true Greek family, but you'll learn more about them later. Once Louis and I were married and our daughter, Antoinette, was old enough to come along we started eating at Amerigo's every few weeks. Dad and daughter soon got hooked on their version of Pasta Carbonera. I think Antoinette loved it because they prepared everything (but the pasta) table side. The tuxedoed waiters whisked raw eggs and freshly grated cheese into a creamy topping for juicy bits of pancetta tossed over fresh pasta.

Alas, Amerigo's closed it's doors making way for an electronics store. Few in the neighborhood seemed to miss it…the era of cocktails and long, festive family dining had come to an end. Everyone was working and rushing and getting take-out.

We have tried ordering Carbonara dishes in many restaurants since then but nothing compares to Amerigo's It wasn't until years later, after we travelled to Italy, that we had a version made just like theirs. I put my own twist on this recipe by adding rosemary. Every so often we enjoy this wonderful simple dish at home (not too often..it is special). Along with pasta we serve it up with a fine wine and lots of great memories.

*Happily Louis Seafood Restaurant is still operating in it's original location, family owned and operated since 1947.

Pasta Carbonera With Rosemary: The Recipe

1 lb ziti or rigatoni pasta
1/2 lb chunk pancetta
2 - 3 eggs
4 tablespoons olive oil
8 oz grated Parmesano Reggiano cheese
2 sprigs fresh rosemary
1 teaspoon sea salt
1 teaspoon fresh ground black pepper

1. Dice pancetta into small bits.
2. In a non-stick skillet add 1 tablespoon olive oil and turn heat on to medium.
3. Add the diced pancetta. Sauté until crisp and brown (be careful not to burn).
4. Set cooked pancetta aside on paper towel to drain.
5. Fill large pot (5 quart) with water and add table salt (about 1 teaspoon). Bring to boil.
6. While water is coming to a boil, remove rosemary leaves from the sprigs and chop finely.
7. In a mixing bowl add 2 eggs and whisk. Add grated cheese. If too thick, add the 3rd egg and mix. Set aside.
8. Add pasta to the boiling water and cook al dente (about 8 - 9 minutes depending on the type of pasta). You want it to have a little bite, not mushy.
9. Prepare serving platter by spooning olive oil on the bottom of a shallow pasta serving dish.
10. Remove cooked pasta from water and transfer immediately to the serving dish. Toss to cover with oil.
11. Pour egg and cheese mixture over the hot pasta and toss well. The heat from the pasta will cook the eggs making a sauce.
12. Toss in the rosemary and mix once more.
13. Garnish with any remaining cheese and rosemary. Top with fresh ground pepper and sea salt.

Note: I use ziti for this dish rather than spaghetti because the pasta mixes more evenly with the cheese and egg sauce. The sauce comes together in a few minutes after your pasta has had a minute or two to sit. If it gets too thick, add a little pasta water.

Main Dish Meatloaf - Dad's Famous Swiss Roll-up

Meatloaf: such a simple dish, there is some type of recipe in almost every culture. In good times and hard times, it is a real comfort food. My dad loved trying all kinds of things in the kitchen. Sometimes he got a little too creative, with some pretty unusual results, but it was always fun tasting everything. My cousin Johnny still talks wildly about his stuffed hamburgers.

One of his most successful ventures was the meatloaf swiss roll. It's ground beef and seasonings flattened out. Then mashed potatoes are added on top of the meat and all are carefully rolled up. All the flavors from the meat mix into the potatoes and it is really delicious. Kids love it because it looks so fun and parents love it because it's a virtual one dish supper. We love it because it takes us back every time we eat it.

You can adjust your seasonings according to your taste. You may use freshly mashed potatoes or dry, packaged ones. It's really up to you. This recipe goes pretty far back (just about the time packaged potatoes were coming out) so we keep with our tradition and always use fresh mashed.

This recipe makes plenty and makes for great leftovers!

The Recipe: Swiss Roll-up Meat Loaf

3 lbs ground beef (You can use ground turkey or chicken. If you do use these, note that they may be a bit sticky when you roll. Wet your hands during this process.)
1 finely chopped onion
2 eggs
1/2 cup Italian breadcrumbs (or non-flavored if you prefer)
1 tablespoon ketchup
1 teaspoon mustard
1 tablespoon Worcestershire sauce
1 teaspoon salt
1 teaspoon pepper
1 1/2 cups cooked mashed potatoes (cooled)

1. Preheat oven to 350 degrees.
2. On clean, dry surface place layer of wax paper or plastic wrap large enough to contain your meat (about 18" or so).
3. Mix the meat thoroughly with all ingredients. If the meat seems a bit dry, add a dash of milk or another egg. In this case you don't want the loaf to be really loose.
4. Spread the meat on the wax paper surface forming it into a large rectangle about 1/2" thick.
5. Spread the cooled mashed potatoes over the meat leaving about 1" around all the edges uncoated.
6. Carefully roll the meat over and over forming the "Swiss Roll."
7. Carefully transfer the roll into a shallow baking pan or onto a sheet pan.

8. Bake for 40 minutes. Let stand about 5 minutes before cutting so that the potatoes and juices all set up.

You can make a gravy using the pan drippings. As kids we just loved topping it with ketchup. It's all up to you and what you enjoy.

No gourmet presumptions in this one, just honest to goodness comfort. Thanks for the memories, Dad.

Bacon Cheeseburger Meat Loaf

Here's another favorite - taking all the flavors of your favorite burger and putting them together in a loaf. One Sunday I had a "Meat Loaf Bake Off" with my daughter and her family. I made Dad's Swiss Roll, Antoinette's Birthday Loaf, and this one. My grandkids noted this one their favorite. True American boys, they love their burgers, in any shape or form!

I don't use any extra salt in this recipe because there is plenty in the cheese and the bacon. Feel free to adjust seasonings as you like. I also try to mimic the flavors of the cheeseburger, not adding too many other ingredients. You want to keep the texture of this more like a burger.

The Recipe: Bacon Cheeseburger Meatloaf

3 lbs ground beef
1 8 oz stick of cheddar cheese
1/2 lb regular sliced bacon
2 eggs
1/2 cup breadcrumbs
1 teaspoon salt
1 teaspoon pepper
2 tablespoons ketchup plus 1/4 cup
1 tablespoon mayonaise

1. In a large bowl mix all ingredients except for the bacon, cheese, and 1/4 cup ketchup.
2. Preheat oven to 350.
3. Cut cheese stick in 1/2 lengthwise.
4. Take 1/2 of meat mixture and place in baking dish large enough to hold loaf but leaving room along the sides. Shape into loaf with flat surface on top.
5. Leaving about 1/2 " on ends, arrange cheese stick in th loaf, pressing it firmly into the meat.
6. Take the remaining meat mixture and place on top of the cheese stick, covering it entirely and sealing loaf ends and sides by pressing the meat together.
7. Brush top of loaf with the 1/4 cup ketchup.
8. Take bacon slices and arrange over loaf in rows or lattice pattern.
9. Place in oven and bake for about 35 - 40 minutes until bacon is fully browned and loaf is firm to the touch.
10. Let stand for about 10 minutes before cutting.

Note: If you use a lattice pattern for your bacon, you will find that using a serrated knife makes cutting easier. When you cut the loaf, the cheese will want to run out. I place a cake slicer on one side while slicing so that it holds the cheese in place. Each slice should have bacon and cheese.

Dijon Garlic Roast Leg of Lamb on Herb Rack

Ahh, here is a Sunday/holiday dish that reflects my mother's taste. She loved lamb. Like most of her generation, lamb was served on Easter Sunday and always with that awesome, bright green mint jelly. I really liked that jelly, I will admit.

In the early 80's, thanks to a great ad campaign, I, and most of the U.S., was introduced to the joy's of Dijon mustard. This mustard packed so much flavor that I began using it instead of the mint jelly. I didn't have a roasting pan with a rack, so I started using celery stalks and other herbs as racks so that the meat would not touch the pan bottom and burn. Don't try using carrots (I did). They have too much sugar and THEY burn!

The great thing about this lamb roast is that all the outer fat is removed. You seal in the juices by brushing the leg with the dijon mixture. It is delicious. You can use that mixture for chops, kabobs, or even as a condiment for burgers.

The recipe: Dijon Garlic Leg of Lame with Herb Rack

1 whole leg of lamb (about 5 pounds)
1 cup dijon mustard
1 tablespoon olive oil
4 cloves garlic peeled and chopped
2 tablespoons fresh rosemary, finey chopped
1 tablespoon sea salt
1 tablespoon coarse ground black pepper
2 stalks celery
4 - 6 rosemary springs

Preheat oven to 350

1. Prepare lamb by using a sharp knife to cut off all the excess outer fat.
2. Rub leg with salt and pepper.
3. In bowl, mix olive oil, mustard, rosemary, and garlic to make a paste.
4. Brush all surfaces of the lamb leg.
5. Take the celery stalks and rosemary and place in your roasting pan to form a rack for the lamb.
6. Place lamb on rack and roast uncovered for 15 minutes per pound.

Let stand for about 15 minutes before carving.

Cutting off all the excess fat makes this a deliciously lean roast. I first made it for Christmas dinner when our daughter was about 10 years old. She (not a really adventurous eater) loved it! Enjoy.

Mom's Sunday Vinegar Chicken

Believe it or not, there was a time when Sundays were truly days of rest, when families and friends could gather together at each other's homes. In our Italian background, Sunday meals always started at 2:00pm. Your mornings were spent at church, relaxing over the newspaper and reading the comics. Around 11:00 or so, the kitchen began to hum. Yes, we often had the traditional red sauce Sunday meals, but my mom always liked to put her own spin on things. This vinegar chicken is one such dish. I remember the tangy aroma of the baking chicken and herbs winding its way upstairs to my room. The tart vinegar in the air made your taste buds burst in anticipation. You bake this dish longer and slower than you would think. The result is juicy, tender chicken. The perfect dish to take center stage on your Sunday (or any day) dining table. It keeps wonderfully well in the frig. Leftovers are yummy.

The Recipe: Vinegar Chicken

1 Whole fryer cut up (I either have the butcher do it or cut it myself). This is the way I do it: 2 drumsticks, 2 thighs, 2 wings (tips removed), 2 breasts (cut each in half giving you 4 total). You may also use the back and neck if you enjoy them.
1 cup red wine vinegar (white is okay as well but we always used red wine vinegar in our house growing up). Have 1 cup on reserve to add during cooking if needed.
10 cloves garlic coarsely chopped
1 bay leaf
1 tablespoon salt
2 tablespoons olive oil

1. Wash the chicken pieces and pat dry with paper towel.
2. In large bowl add chicken, olive oil, salt and pepper, and red wine. Mix together making sure that all the chicken gets coated.
3. Preheat oven to 350.
4. Place chicken in shallow roasting pan large enough so that you do not overcrowd the pieces. Place the bay leaf in the pan.
5. Sprinkle the chopped garlic all over the chicken.
6. Bake chicken in oven at 350 for 30 minutes. Baste pan juices over chicken, continue baking 30 minutes more. If juices have evaporated, add more vinegar to the pan. This will become your new pan juices. Baste after 15 minutes.
7. At this point chicken should be done. Raise heat in oven to 400. If you need to add more vinegar do so at this point. Place pan back in over and cook on this temperature for 5 to 10 minutes to brown up chicken.

Remove from baking pan and place on serving platter spooning juices over the chicken. This dish is great paired with rice or oven roasted potatoes and a nice green salad.

Christmas Eve Anchovy Bread

Yes, by now you know we are very Italian; and being so, meant Christmas Eve was time for the Feast of The Seven Fishes! No one really knows why it is seven fishes, but we sure enjoyed all the wonderful seafood variations.

So this brings us to the often maligned member of the seafood family, the anchovy. Like liver, you either love 'em or hate 'em. My mom and dad loved them and I am happy to say that I love them too. My sister was never really a fan and my husband, Louis, never ate them at all until long after we were married. He loves them now. This simple recipe is made with just a few ingredients. It takes very little time and packs a big flavor punch. Give it a try. I promise you, you will probably have to make two. Every time I serve this, if flies right off the plate. I serve it with a dish of marinara sauce for dipping.

The Recipe: Anchovy Bread

1 ball fresh pizza dough (you can find this in the bakery section of your supermarket, or buy some at your local pizzeria). In a pinch you can use the canned refrigerated dough, but that is a bit sweeter than traditional pizza dough.
1 can flat fillets of anchovies in olive oil
4 oz. mozzarella (sliced)
4 leaves fresh basil
1 - 2 tablespoons sesame seeds (depending on your taste)
1 egg white
2 tablespoons coarse corn meal
Flour for your rolling surface
Parchment paper

1. Get a large bowl that will accommodate your size of pizza dough. Spray bottom and sides with cooking spray. (If you don't want use spray, you can use olive oil.)
2. Remove dough from package and place in the bowl. Spray the crown of the ball with cooking spray (or rub with olive oil to prevent sticking. Cover dough with clean kitchen towel or plastic wrap.
3. Place in un-heated oven to let rise. You may also set it out on your counter. Dough should rise in a few hours to double its size. I often prepare dough the night before and then it's all set when I am ready to begin work in the morning.
4. Flour your surface for rolling out the dough. You may also want to flour your rolling pin.
5. Remove dough from bowl and pound the air out. Knead the dough until pliable and easy to manipulate.
6. Use your rolling pin and roll out the dough into a rectangular shape. You may find that you can use your hands to help this process.

7. Keep in mind that you will want to leave about a 1" space at the top of your roll free of any filling. Also make sure not go all the way to the sides. Place anchovy filets along the top 1/3 of your roll.
8. Add your mozzarella slices directly beneath them. Don't overfill.
9. Tear your basil leaves and spread over entire filing area.
10. Now it's time to roll: use a firm hand when doing this so that you pack in the filling. Starting at the top of the roll using both hands, roll layer over layer until you reach the bottom. Keeping the roll seam side down.
11. Make sure roll is secure and seal each end by pinching dough together.
12. Beat the egg white and brush top of roll.
13. Sprinkle sesame seeds along top (as much as you like).
14. Take a sheet pan and line it with parchment paper.
15. Sprinkle corn meal on parchment surface.
16. Carefully transfer roll onto your baking sheet.
17. Bake for 15 to 20 minutes at 400 degrees until top is lightly golden and firm to touch.
18. Let cool for about 5 minutes before slicing.

Don't let the rolling process discourage you from making this. Everyone loves it! You can do so many variations with this recipe. For those who don't like anchovies, use any fillings you like: pepperoni, sausage, roasted cauliflower, sun-dried tomatoes…use your imagination.

Mashed Potato Pie

My sister, Donna is famous for this dish. Every holiday it finds its way onto her table. I don't know of anyone who doesn't go crazy about it. It really is a great dish for the busy holiday times because you can prepare it ahead. I don't know where she first found this dish, but I am certainly glad that she did!

The recipe: Mashed Potato Pie

(This recipe is made for the big holiday crowd. You can adjust to smaller amounts to suit your occasion.)

5 lbs potatoes (boiled and mashed)
1/2 lb butter
1 cup grated parmesan cheese
1 lb mozzarella
salt and pepper to taste
2 tablespoons chopped parsley
1/4 cup breadcrumbs
butter or cooking spray for pan

1. Mix potatoes with butter, grated cheese, salt and pepper, and parsley.
2. Grease a large baking pan (about 9 x 13) with butter or cooking spray.
3. Coat bottom of pan with breadcrumbs.
4. Add one layer of mashed potatoes to pan covering the bottom.
5. Add layer of thick sliced mozzarella (1//4") over potatoes.
6. Continue alternating between potatoes and cheese ending with potatoes.
7. Sprinkle top layer with grated cheese.

Bake in 350 oven for 30 minutes, until top is crusty and browned.

Salads Aside

One thing you could always count on having with dinners at our house was some type of salad. Some families would eat the salads first, others along with their meal, and some even at the end. When I was growing up in the 50's and 60's, the salad's main character was good old ice berg lettuce. My mom's every day salad was lettuce, tomato and oil and vinegar dressing. True to the era, convenience for the "homemaker" was a really big deal. TV dinners, popcorn in it's own foil pan, and voila - bottled salad dressing! Everyone wanted to try new things, and what a novelty it was to top your blank canvas of a salad with Green Goddess or even Thousand Island! Although these bottled dressings were not better than fresh made, they were fun and certainly got a lot more kids and families eating their greens.

I am happy to say that our daughter and her family still have salads with almost every meal, and that they still sit down to family dinners. Our tastes have evolved from the iceberg, branching out to the rich, leafy greens like kale, spinach and arugula. Salads today include all matter of add-ins: eggs, meats, cheeses, etc. Beets have become really popular these days. In these two recipes, the BEET is the star of the show.

Beet and Onion Salad

I first had the Beet and Onion salad as a young girl, around 10 years old. My friend, Denise's grandparents were very traditional Italian. One Saturday I was going to go to the beach with Denise and her family. The beach was out on Long Island. Usually we left early and came back around dinner time. I remember being in her grandparent's basement kitchen helping to prepare our sandwiches for the day: scrambled eggs on crisp rolls. Of course you had to have some vegetable. That's where the beets came in. I loved the tart taste of the vinegar and the salt.

The recipe: Beet and Onion Salad (Version 1)

2 cans regular cut beets, drained
1 small onion, sliced
1 tablespoon salt
1 teaspoon dried oregano
2 tablespoons olive oil

1. Use a mixing bowl; add beets, onion and gently toss.
2. Add vinegar, salt and pepper, then the olive oil.
3. Taste: should be tangy and a little salty. Adjust to your taste.
4. Add the dried oregano, toss all ingredients.
5. Transfer to serving bowl.
6. Chill for at least 30 minutes before serving. (Just before serving, taste salad to see if the flavors have developed. Adjust according to your liking.)

Beet and Onion Salad (Version 2)

The recipe: Roasted Beet and Onion Salad with Beet Greens

1 bunch fresh beets, stems and greens attached
1 medium onion, peeled and quartered
1 tablespoon salt
1 teaspoon black pepper
2 sprigs rosemary
1/4 cup olive oil
3 tablespoons balsamic vinegar
2 tablespoons fresh chopped parsley

1. Prepare the beets for roasting.
    1. Cut beet tops (greens) from the beet root
    2. Rinse greens thoroughly and let drain in colander
    3. Scrub each beet root making sure to remove any stubborn soil.
    4. Set aside to dry on paper towel.
    5. Cover your work counter with newspaper so that you won't have beet juice staining your area. Peel the beats. Using a cutting board, cut beets into quarters or smaller depending on the size of your root.
    6. Place the beets in a mixing bowl.
    7. Take the beet tops and cut the green leafs from the stems.
    8. Place the leafy greens back in the colander. Discard your newspaper covering and clean your work surface.
2. Preheat oven to 350.
3. Add your prepared onions to the beets in the mixing bowl.
4. Add the olive oil and toss the vegetables, coating all.
5. In shallow baking pan, spread vegetables evenly. Sprinkle with salt and pepper.
6. Place rosemary spring on top of the vegetables and place pan in oven.
7. Roast for 30 minutes. Beets should be firm but your knife should be able to run through.
8. Take your beet greens and coarsely chop, place in mixing bowl
9. Taking oil from your roasting pan, add to the greens and lightly toss.
10. Toss in the cooked beets and onions with the greens. The greens will wilt due to the heat of the vegetables.
11. Add the balsamic vinegar and toss again.
12. Turn salad into serving bowl and top with fresh chopped parsley.

Aunt Ida's Ricotta Cake

My mom's family came from Rochester, in Upstate New York. Today it's just a quick commuter flight away, but growing up when I did, no one had the money or time to make the trip very often. It was really exciting whenever these visits happened. Every few summers the Di Guillio clan would make the long road trip down to our home in The Bronx. We'd have barbecues in our backyard. Uncle Sam loved to play guitar and sing. We'd sit in the living room around my mom's piano and just enjoy. Very simple stuff…the stuff of memories. Some years after Uncle Sam passed away I made the trip up to visit Aunt Ida, along with my husband, Louis and my sister, Donna. We gathered at Aunt Ida's; sitting around her living room, just chatting with our cousins. True to our Italian tradition, Aund Ida had prepared a big feast of lasagna and meatballs. The "icing on the cake" was a pure and simple ricotta cake Aunt Ida had been making for years and years. While a lot of cooks today scoff at using boxed cake mixes, my mom and those of her generation were thrilled with the coming of these time saving wonders. Our childhoods were peppered with new-fangled goodies like these. What fun! Don't turn up your nose at the boxed recipe. It comes with a special ingredient at the end…a touch of love.

(Note: Aunt Ida used cake mix with "pudding in the mix." I have not found these available for some time. No matter, I have always used a good yellow cake mix and it comes out just great.)

The recipe: Aunt Ida's Ricotta Cake

1 box yellow cake mix (see package for additional ingredients)
2 pounds ricotta cheese
1/2 cup sugar
4 eggs (beaten)
1 teaspoon vanilla
   FOR THE TOPPING
4 teaspoons sugar
1/2 teaspoon cinnamon

1. Preheat oven to 350.
2. Butter and flour cake pan (9 x 13).
3. In large mixing bowl prepare cake mix according to mix.
4. Mix together in separate bowl: ricotta, eggs, sugar and vanilla.
5. Pour cake mix batter into cake pan.
6. Spoon ricotta mixture on TOP of cake batter. Do not mix together.
7. Bake about 60 minutes.
8. Make topping by mixing together sugar and cinnamon.
9. When cake is done, remove from oven and sprinkle with the topping while hot.
10. Cool in refrigerator. Best served chilled.

This is one of the best cakes ever!

Aunt Rose's Pumpkin Bread

My father's brother, Uncle Joe, moved out to St. Louis when we were very young. I never knew him well because they were so far away. Happily through social media I am close my dear cousins, Carole, Linda and Barbara.

Some years ago, Barbara gave me a call. Seems she had been speaking with our Aunt Ann (dad's sister) about how hard it was see each other. Auntie Ann told her that we girls better do something about that before it's too late! Enough of just seeing each other for funerals or other sad occasions..get together to celebrate life.

And so we did! Girl Cousins Weekend in St. Louis happened and we all had a wonderful time. As part of the weekend, we each bought a small gift for all the cousins representing something about themselves, or where they were living. Just a trinket, a way to share. I brought a seashell candle (we live near the Gulf in Florida), cousin-in-law Cheri bought a beautiful sample of granite native to her Michigan home. Cousin Linda bought us each a small loaf of her Aunt Rose's Pumpkin Bread (and gave each of us the recipe). What a great idea! We had such a blast that weekend, making memories that will last a lifetime.

This recipe is so easy to make. A happy note to any weight watchers out there..the last time I made it, in my haste, I forgot to add the vegetable oil! I figured I'd bake it anyway and, low and behold, it was awesome. Just bake it a few minutes longer.

The Recipe: Aunt Rose's Pumpkin Bread

Makes 3 standard size loaves

3 1/3 cups flour
3 cups sugar
1 1/2 teaspoon salt
2 teaspoons baking soda
2 teaspoons pumpkin pie spice (or nutmeg)
2 teaspoons cinnamon
1 cup vegetable oil
2/3 cup water
4 eggs
2 cups pumpkin
(optional) 1 cup chopped walnuts or raisins

1. Preheat oven to 375.
2. Grease and flour 3 loaf pans
3. Sift together all dry ingredients (except the nuts or raisins).
4. Thoroughly stir in all the wet ingredients (I used a hand mixer on low).

5. Add nuts or raisins and blend through.
6. Fill pans just a bit over 1/2 full.
7. Bake for 45 minutes.

This loaf keeps very well in the refrigerator. It is delicious served with a bit of fresh whipped cream. I have also made it using both raisins and nuts, just 1/2 cup of each.

Donna's Beauty Shoppe Carrot Cake

You can pick up lots of great information at the local beauty shop. My sister, Donna got this recipe from a hairdresser she worked with in a shop called Jean and Bertha's in Throgg's Neck, The Bronx. She was an old-fashioned German woman who really knew her stuff when it came to making great comfort desserts. I got this recipe from Donna about 30 (yikes!) years ago. It just goes to show you that, once a classic, always a classic. I made it most recently for a friend's birthday - same ingredients, same method. Everyone loved it. It's moist and full of color from the freshly shredded carrots. The cream cheese frosting is worth every calorie. Hey, we don't do this every day!!

The recipe: Donna's Beauty Shoppe Carrot Cake

2 cups flour
2 cups sugar
2 teaspoons baking soda (don't need if using cake flour)
2 teaspoons cinnamon
1 teaspoon salt
1 cup vegetable oil
1 teaspoon vanilla
4 eggs
3 cups shredded carrots
  FOR THE FROSTING
1/2 lb. butter - softened
8 oz. cream cheese - softened
16 oz. confectioners sugar
1 teaspoon vanilla
(Optional) 1 cup pecans (chopped)

1. Preheat oven to 375.
2. Grease and flour 2 9" cake pans.
3. In large mixing bowl beat eggs and sugar.
4. Add vegetable oil, cinnamon, salt, vanilla and carrots - blend.
5. Add flour and baking soda. Blend all ingredients using hand mixer on low.
6. Pour into prepared cake pans.
7. Bake about 30 minutes.
8. Place cakes on racks to cool while preparing frosting.
9. To make frosting - in mixing bowl blend softened cream cheese, butter and vanilla.
10. Add confectioners sugar and blend a little at a time until all ingredients are blended thoroughly.
11. If using nuts, fold into frosting mixture.
12. Once cake has cooled frost top half on one cake. Layer second cake on top of frosted one. Frost top and sides of cake.

This cake is best when made the day before and kept refrigerated. It is a "ta da!" kind of cake. It makes a great entrance, perfect for a special party, but why not go ahead, bake it and make any day a special one.

Baked Stuffed Artichokes
Recipe Page: 8

Marinara Sauce
Recipe Page: 11

Pasta Carbonera With Rosemary
Recipe Page: 14

Bacon Cheeseburger Meatloaf
Recipe Page: 18

Beet and Onion Salad
Recipe Page: 24

Aunt Rose's Pumpkin Bread
Recipe Page: 27

SECTION IA
The Greek Connection

I met my husband, Louis, as a teenager. He was friends with my friend's brother! I kind of always felt something special about him, but, who could guess how things turned out? What a blast we have had. What fun merging our families together. Louis's was the first Greek family I knew. Now, some 40 plus years later, I can't even begin to number the amount of friends and family we consider a part of our lives. Blood cousins, "Village" cousins, Uncles, Aunts, nieces, nephews…on and on it goes. Here is a little bit about how it started.

My mother-in-law, Eleni Loucas Kikis, came over to the United States via steamer ship in the mid-1940's. She was newly married (just over one year). Her husband, Nick, left their home country of Cyprus shortly after their marriage to seek his fortune in America. Eleni made the arduous 6 week journey by herself, carrying with her her first born child, 6 month old John. She spoke no English and was just 20 years old. The pair arrived in New York City safe and sound but pretty much isolated on an island of millions.

Nick had arrived in New York by way of South America entering through Ellis Island. He spoke fluent Spanish (earning him the nickname - Nick the Spaniard) and had a good command of English. He worked in diners in Hell's Kitchen where the couple and their young baby set up their first apartment.

Shortly after arriving in the states Eleni and Nick had a second son, Louis. The young family now needed a larger place to live. They found an apartment uptown in Harlem on West 135th Street. It was walking distance to Riverside Park, where Eleni would spend long afternoons with her boys while Nick spent long days working in area restaurants.

There in Riverside park groups of young mothers, like Eleni, found themselves drawn to the familiar sounds of the language of the "old country." The small groups shared all sorts of tips on childcare, gossip, and memories over many an afternoon. Among them they found strengths and weaknesses. Who was the best seamstress? Who knew how to cure a cold? Who knew the best Greek-speaking doctors? Where to shop? How to cook? And so it came to be that these ladies and their families forged friendships that would last their entire lives.

Nick and Eleni would have one of the most popular households. Nick was gracious host who welcomed all the new arrivals into his home. It seemed there was always someone sleeping on the fold-out sofa. Most evenings and Sundays after church friends and family gathered for coffee, brandy and pastries. Ravanie cake and Galatoboureka (phyllo custard pie) were clear favorites then and they remain so today. Eleni got her recipes from her friends in the park handmade them her own. She learned her baking skills well, At age 83 she was still able to bake up pan after pan of her specialties for the annual church bazaar. Now we bake these wonderful treats with her in mind.

A note on these recipes: they have been translated from Greek to English and from metric measurements to our own. I was lucky enough to have baked them side-by-side with Eleni and she did her best to get the measurements right. In the photo section of this book you'll see a picture of Eleni's tiny hand-written recipe book.

Pan-fried Halloumi Cheese - a wonderful appetizer or snack

Halloumi is a semi-hard, unripened brined cheese from Northern Cyprus, the section of the island where our family hails from. It is only produced in Cyprus for import throughout the world. This cheese has a high melting point, which lends it beautifully to frying and grilling. In the villages, during the summer months, the favorite way to enjoy this salty cheese is chilled and eaten along with sweet, juicy watermelon.

The story of Halloumi is not merely the history of a type of cheese, it represents deep-rooted memories for an entire generation of displaced people. Here's our story.

In 1974 Turkey invaded Cyprus and took control of the Northern part. This included Eleni and Nick's home town of Eptakomi, in the Famagusta district. At this time there were still many relatives living there. Following the occupation the Greek-Cypriots were expelled from the sector and, thus they had now become refugees. They left their homes with what little they could carry, some very young, some very old, all homeless.

Our relatives were very lucky. They had family (both blood and "village") in the United States, and also in England. There were even some spread as far away as Australia. Throughout the middle and late seventies we welcomed them into our homes and communities, helping them find homes, get jobs, and enroll in school.

Every time we get together, you are sure to find Halloumi on the table in some form; and then the stories begin to flow. This simple dish of fried cheese and lemon reminds us of times past. It is the heart and sole of our family on a plate.

The recipe: Pan-fried Halloumi Cheese with Lemon

1 8 oz package of Halloumi
4 tablespoons olive oil (enough to cover your pan, you don't want to deep fry)
2 lemons (1 cut in serving wedges, one for juicing)
1 teaspoon dried mint

1. Prepare the cheese: remove from package, rinse and pat dry thoroughly with paper towel.
2. Slice cheese into about 1/4" pieces. You will see that this cheese seems to be folded in half. Often you will see dried mint in the center. Cut cheese lengthwise so that you keep both halves of the cheese in tact.
3. Heat the olive oil in pan until it bubbles when you drop a bit of water in it. I prefer a non-stick pan but cast iron works well too.
4. Place the cheese slices in the pan, making sure to leave enough space for turning. The cheese will cook very fast. By the time you finish laying out the slices, you will be ready to turn the first one and so on.

5. Once all slices have been cooked on both sides, remove from pan and transfer on to serving plate.
6. Spoon a bit of the olive oil over the cheese and then squeeze the lemon juice over it.
7. Sprinkle the cheese with the dried mint.

Serve the cheese with a slice of lemon on the side. The olive oil and lemon juice are a great pairing with this salty cheese. Enjoy a bit of our history.

Greek Meatballs (Keftedes)

What makes these meatballs unique is the addition of grated potato and ground cinnamon. I make mine using ground chicken, but they are traditionally made with lamb. You may also use ground beef.

The first time I had these was very early on in my marriage. My husband, Louis, wanted to show me a little bit of his Greek heritage and try out his cooking skills. I was working that particular day, so coming home to a cooked meal was certainly welcome.

When I walked in the door, I got a real surprise! Those little meatballs had given Louis a bit of trouble. Seems he'd just used ground meat, rolled them into balls and fried them up. Fried them up a bit too much…he actually was able to bounce one off the floor! I don't know how, but we managed to eat some, and I remember thinking that there must be a better way. All the Greeks certainly would not like these meatballs!

Well, shortly thereafter, while at my mother-in-law, Eleni's, house, I found out I was right. She was making keftedes. I watched her grating the potato and onion. She was making a ton of these for a party. She grated so much onion, the air was pungent with the odor and it made our eyes tear! None of that mattered when those cute little meatballs started coming out of her pan, beautifully browned and so moist and delicious. Aha..so that's how it was done!

The recipe: Greek Meatballs (Keftedes)

1 lb ground meat (chicken, lamb, or beef)
1 small onion (grated)
1 small potato (grated)
1 teaspoon cinnamon
1 teaspoon salt
1 teaspoon pepper
salt and pepper for seasoning the dredging flour
1 teaspoon dried mint (you can use fresh, but make sure to chop fine
1 egg
1/4 cup breadcrumbs
1 cup flour for dredging
1 cup vegetable oil

1. In mixing bowl combine meat, potato and onion. Gently mix together.
2. Add the dried mint, cinnamon, salt, pepper and egg.
3. Mix all ingredients together. If too moist, add a bit of breadcrumbs. If too dry, add additional egg.
    PREPARE YOUR AREA FOR DREDGING
4. Put flour in a shallow pan (I use a pie plate). Season with salt and pepper.

5. Have one plate for your uncoated meatballs, one for the coated ones, and one for the cooked ones. Line the final plate with a paper towel to absorb any excess cooking oil.
6. Have a glass of water and a teaspoon ready. Now get rolling. Take the teaspoon and dip it in the water. Using the spoon, take meat from the mixing bowl and roll it into a ball. Place that ball onto the plate for dredging. Continue rolling all the balls until the meat is used up.
7. For dredging, I find it easy to use 2 forks and take the keftedes one by one, roll them in the flour to LIGHTLY coat. Transfer coated balls onto the next plate. Continue until all the balls are coated.
8. Heat the oil and get ready for some frying. I don't deep fry. As with the Halloumi, I find that, by the time I put in a number of meatballs, the first ones are ready to be turned. Watch your heat, keep it on medium so that they don't cook too quickly. I usually do batches of 12 at a time. Once browned on all sides, transfer to the final plate and salt each batch as soon as they come out.
9. Transfer the keftedes to serving platter.

If you make these, beware, they will be a big hit and fly off your plate. Word to the wise, make plenty of extra. They are great at room temperature served with a squeeze of lemon. You can also serve with a dipping sauce made from combining a cup of Greek yogurt and grated cucumber, or dill.

Stuffed Grape Leaves (2 Varieties)

The custom of wrapping food in grape leaves goes back over centuries. Most cultures have some form of stuffed leaves or vegetables. Cabbage, tomatoes, zucchini, eggplant, you name it, there is probably a recipe for stuffing it!

While my mother made stuffed cabbage and stuffed peppers, growing up in our neighborhood, with mostly Italian and Irish households, we never even dreamed of eating stuffed grape leaves. Oh, we used to sneak over to my next door neighbor's house at night as kids and pick a few grapes from her vine, but we never thought about eating them!

The first time I ate grape leaves, (dolmathes is the Greek word; koupipia is the Cypriot word) they were at Eleni's home. She made the traditional meat and rice stuffed leaves. It seemed that when she decided to make these it would become a stuffing day. She would make big batches of vine leaves and big batches of cabbage leaves too. Yum.

Early on she rarely made the dolmathes stuffed only with rice. This version usually came out on feast days when you were not allowed to eat meat. They are really tasty and a nice change. I like to make the rice version for my vegetarian friends. I add currents or golden raisins and pine nuts.

The recipe: Stuffed Grape Leaves (2 varieties)

For either version you need:
1 jar brined grape leaves (remove from jar and rinse under cold water)
1 medium onion (minced)
1 cup olive oil
1 1/2 cup long grain rice (for the RICE version)
    or 1 cup long grain rice for the MEAT
1/2 cup chopped, fresh dil
1 1/2 teaspoon salt
1/2 teaspoon black pepper
Juice of 2 lemons
 FOR THE MEAT
1 8 oz can tomato sauce
1 teaspoon cinnamon
1 pound ground beef
 FOR THE RICE
1 teaspoon dried mint
1/2 cup pine nuts
1/4 cup currents (if desired)

MEAT
1. Prepare the filling: combine the meat, dill, tomato sauce and mix.
2. Add the onion, juice of 1 lemon, salt, pepper and rice.
3. Add 1/4 cup olive oil and mix everything well by hand.
4. Line bottom of heavy saucepan with grape leaves (use broken ones, there are usually a few in each jar)
5. Begin rolling the dolma: On a flat surface place a grape leaf with the stem toward you, underside of leaf is face up.
6. Cut off the stem of the leaf and overlap the bottom part of the leaf toward the center.
7. Place a table spoon of filling in the bottom center of the leaf just above the stem.
8. Fold the bottom section up to cover the filling.
9. Fold the sides toward the center and continue rolling until you are at the top of the leaf. Rolls should be firm but not tight as the filling will expand during cooking.
10. Place the rolled leaf in the saucepan, seam side down.
11. Continue rolling the leaves. Place them the saucepan packing them tightly.
12. When rolling is completed, pour 1/2 cup olive oil over the mixture along with juice of 1 lemon.
13. Cover the rolls with any remaining leaves.
14. Fill saucepan with enough water (you can use chicken broth) to cover the rolls.
15. Place an inverted, heat-proof plate on top of the rolls to weight them down.
16. Cover the saucepan and bring to a boil.
17. Lower the heat and continue cooking on low for about 30 minutes until the rice filling is cooked and the leaves are tender. (I keep the saucepan covered after turning off the heat until the pot has cooled. This ensures that the leaves are tender.)

RICE
1. In a large skillet, over medium heat olive oil (about 1/2 cup).
2. Stir in the onions and cook until translucent.
3. Add the pine nuts, rice, dill, mint, salt and pepper.
4. Remove from heat. Stir in the lemon juice and allow to cool.
5. FOLLOW STEPS FOR MEAT from step 5 through 17.

Hint: Once you have covered your saucepan and lowered the heat, give it a good shake to make sure the leaves are not sticking. If you have an electric stove (as I do) keep the heat on low so that the bottom leaves don't burn. If the cooking process is complete and your leaves are not done, no problem, just add a bit more liquid, heat the pot again, cover tightly and let sit. It will gently steam and be just fine.

Moussaka (Baked Eggplant Casserole)

Don't shy away from trying this recipe. It is easy to follow, makes wonderful leftovers and makes you look like a kitchen rock star.

The recipe: Moussaka

  FOR THE MEAT SAUCE
2 tablespoons butter
1 medium onion, chopped
1 1/2 pound ground meat (beef or lamb)
1 clove garlic, crushed
1/2 teaspoon dried oregano
1 teaspoon dried basil
1 teaspoon cinnamon
1 teaspoon salt
dash black pepper
2 8oz cans tomato sauce
  FOR THE BÉCHAMEL CREAM SAUCE
2 tablespoons butter
2 tablespoons flour
1/2 teaspoon salt
dash black pepper
2 cups milk or half and half
2 eggs
  OTHER INGREDIENTS
2 eggplants, about 1 lb in size washed and dried

1/2 cup butter (melted)*
1/2 cup parmesan cheese, grated
1/2 cup cheddar cheese, grated
2 tablespoons breadcrumbs

1. Meat Sauce: Melt butter in 3 1/2 quart saucepan.
2. Add onion, meat, and garlic, stirring until meat is brown (about 10 minutes).
3. Add herbs, spices and tomato sauce.
4. Bring to boil while stirring.
5. Reduce heat and simmer for 1/2 hour.
6. Prepare the eggplants: Halve unpeeled eggplants lengthwise. Cut each half crosswise into 1/2 inch slices.
7. Spray cookie sheet or sheet pan with cooking spray.
8. Place slices side by side in rows on cookie tray, sprinkle lightly with salt and pepper.

9. *I use olive oil cooking spray instead of butter here. Brush each slice lightly with melted butter.
10. Place cookie sheet in oven and bake about 5 minutes until eggplant slices are softened and turning lightly golden.
11. Remove from pan and set aside.
12. Make Béchamel sauce: In medium saucepan melt butter and remove from heat.
13. Stir in flour, salt and pepper.
14. Add milk gradually, stirring as you go. Bring to boil and keep stirring until mixture thickens. Remove from heat.
15. In small bowl beat eggs with wire whisk. Add a small amount of the hot cream sauce and whisk. Gradually add a bit more hot mixture until your egg mixture is warm, stirring as you go.
16. Add this warm mixture to the balance of the cream sauce in the saucepan. Stir all together and set aside.
17. Assemble the casserole: Preheat oven to 350.
18. In shallow 2 quart baking dish (about 12" x 12" x 2) layer half the eggplant, overlapping slightly.
19. Sprinkle 2 tablespoons each grated parmesan and cheddar cheese.
20. Stir breadcrumbs into meat sauce.
21. Spoon meat sauce evenly over eggplant layer.
22. Continue layering as before until all eggplant is used up, ending with meat sauce layer (save some cheese for topping).
23. Pour cream sauce over entire casserole and sprinkle on any remaining cheese.
24. Bake 35 to 40 minutes or until golden brown and top is set.
25. Cool about 15 minutes before serving to allow all flavors and ingredients to settle.

Variations: Alternate layers of eggplant and potatoes. Substitute zucchini for eggplant.

Galatoboureka (phyllo custard pie)

The recipe: Galatoboureka (phyllo custard pie)

Note on using phyllo - You can easily cut the sheets to fit your pan. Work quickly as it dries out fast. If you will be taking a long time or get interrupted, cover the opened sheets with lightly moistened cloth.

1 1-pound package phyllo sheets
1/2 lb melted unsalted butter
   FOR THE CUSTARD
1 quart milk
8 egg yolks
4 oz sugar
1 cup farina
   FOR THE SYRUP
4 oz orange juice
2 cups sugar
1 cup water
1 cinnamon stick
2 whole cloves

1. Make the custard: in medium saucepan add milk and farina. Stir and add sugar. Stir about 5 minutes on medium heat until creamy. Let cool for 30 minutes. This is important because you don't want to cook the egg yolks. While the mixture cools, beat the egg yolks in bowl until smooth. Add beaten yolks to farina/milk mixture and stir until smooth.
2. Preheat oven to 350. Prepare your baking pan. I use a 16" x 11" lasagna pan. Any size oblong would do. If you have extra mixture, use additional smaller pan.
3. Brush bottom of pan with butter.
4. Layer phyllo: 2 sheets on bottom, brush with butter.
5. Layer remaining half package of phyllo as follows: 2 sheets phyllo, brush top sheet with butter. You'll use about 14 sheets for this process. This will be your base.
6. Add custard mixture evenly over buttered phyllo.
7. Now you are ready for top layering. As you did before, layer phyllo 2 sheets at a time, buttering the top one until the package is used up. Make sure you don't over butter. You'll now want to completely butter the top layer including all sides and corners.
8. Gently roll over edges and corners all around pan. This encloses the custard mixture and keeps the pastry moist inside while baking. Brush with any remaining butter.
9. With sharp knife gently pierce small holes in 3 - 4 rows (depending on the size of your pan) lengthwise and crosswise. This ventilates the pastry.
10. Bake pastry about 20 - 30 minutes until top is golden brown. Remember the filling is already cooked. You are only baking long enough to brown the phyllo.
11. Remove from the oven and set out to cool about 30 minutes.

12. Make the syrup now by adding the sugar, water and other ingredients in a medium saucepan, bringing it to a boil.
13. Allow syrup to cool and slowly pour syrup mixture over entire pastry, allowing it to seep into phyllo.
14. Once pastry is cooled, you prepare to serve by cutting into squares or triangles.

As with Ravanie (the recipe follows this one), you might like to sprinkle cinnamon on top of the pastry. We like to enjoy this pie at room temperature with a cup of rich Greek coffee or espresso. Some people like to have it heated and topped with whipped cream.

Ravanie Cake

This is a deliciously moist sheet cake. The addition of the farina gives the cake a wonderful texture.

The recipe: Ravanie Cake

2 cups coarse farina
1 cup flour
3 teaspoons baking powder
6 eggs
3/4 cups sugar
pinch salt
1/4 cup unsalted butter
8 oz orange juice
1 teaspoon vanilla
2 tablespoons brandy
 FOR THE SYRUP
2 cups syrup
1 cup water
1/2 teaspoon lemon juice
(Optional) 3/4 cup chopped almonds

1. Preheat over to 350.
2. Butter and flour 13" x 9" baking pan*
3. Sift farina, flour, baking powder and salt.
4. Cream butter and sugar in separate bowl.
5. In large mixing bowl, beat eggs with electric mixer.
6. Gradually add butter and sugar mixture to eggs.
7. Add orange juice, vanilla, and brandy to this mixture.
8. Slowly add dry mixture to egg mixture beating until smooth.
9. Turn into prepared baking pan.
10. Bake at 350 for 25 minutes.
11. Raise temperature to 400 and bake additional 10 minutes.
12. Remove from oven and let cool.
13. For syrup: in saucepan add sugar, then water and lemon juice. Stir and bring to boil. Make sure not to over boil as it will become too thick. You want watery consistency.**
14. Remove from heat.
15. Pour hot syrup over cooled cake.
16. If desired sprinkle chopped almonds over entire cake.
17. Cool and cut into squares to serve.

*If you find this recipe too large for your pan, add any extra to a smaller square pan. This recipe was handed down over many years so the pan measurement may have changed. I use a lasagna pan which is a bit larger that the 9" x 13".

**When I first tried baking this cake I overcooked the syrup and it came out like a hard clear shell over the cake. Not a good thing!

I cover my cooled cake with clear plastic wrap after it has been cut into in order to keep it moist. Kids love it. Once you have poured the syrup over the cake, you might like to try adding a sprinkle of cinnamon over the top.

Pan Fried Hallomi Cheese
Recipe Page: 42

Keftedes - Greek Meatballs
Recipe Page: 44

Moussake
Recipe Page: 48

Revanie Cake
Recipe Page: 52

Galatoboureka Pie
Recipe Page: 50

SECTION II

Firehouse Memories

The Brotherhood — Firehouse Tested, Brother Approved

Much has been said about the special bond among members of the New York City Fire Department (FDNY). It is very true that once someone you know becomes one of them, you have an extended family that will be with you for the rest of your life. You'll go to countless company dances, christenings, weddings, graduations and more. Need work done on your home? One call will bring a small construction crew over in minutes flat! You'll take trips together, have picnics together, share in all things good and bad.

My husband, Louis and I were lucky enough to have spent a good portion of our adult lives in this environment. Life as part of the FDNY is truly family life. Like all families there is ribbing, rivalry, competitive spirit, and a good amount of practical joking to boot. Firefighters share the housekeeping chores, including cleaning and cooking those famous firehouse meals. When it is your turn to cook, you had better come up with a crowd pleaser. The pressure is definitely on! Louis enjoyed backyard grilling but, as a young firefighter, he had very little kitchen experience. When his company was buying the meal, he would call me up and ask for quick, easy to prepare meals. They needed to be hearty enough for the most robust appetites and tasty enough for both adventurous and tame palates alike.

Recipes in this section:

Sidor's Fire Starter Peppers
"Tasmanian" Chicken
Red Tide Pot Roast
Firehouse Meatloaf
Ribs on the Run

TASMANIAN CHICKEN

Tastes Just Like Chicken

This recipe goes way back into the mid-70's! It was given to me sister, Donna from her sister-in-law, Rose. It is one of the easiest meals to make and one that has never disappointed. It has moved on far beyond the firehouse, spreading to kitchens as far away as St. Thomas! It is a chicken dish with pasta and peppers. In its purest form the dish calls for boneless chicken breasts; cream of mushroom soup; jarred, pickled (vinegar) peppers; and hot cherry peppers. The pasta used in the original recipe was a long wavy spaghetti called fusilli. The dish didn't have any special name.

After one trip to the firehouse, the vinegar peppers were outmaneuvered by the hot cherry peppers, and any pasta readily available would easily fit the bill. The simple chicken dish became known as Tasmanian Chicken courtesy of Firefighter Dan Duddy's heavy hand with spices. The dish is a curious combination of creamy sauce and vinegary tang from the peppers but it tastes wonderful. Whether you keep the heat under control or stoke the flames with extra peppers, you will definitely enjoy it. The first Tasmanian Chicken was served up in Engine Company 22/Ladder Company 13 over 30 years ago. It's a dish that is as full of life and fun as it ever was, but just like any practical joke, don't take it too seriously. You might not get it at first, but let it sink in a bit and you'll come away smiling.

(Note to any purists out there: I have made this with homemade cream of mushroom soup too. Don't feel you have to use the canned version if you don't want to!)

The recipe: Tasmanian Chicken

This is a very quick dish to prepare. Start by setting up your pasta water (salted) to boil and do the rest of the preparations while it comes up to boil. Everything should be ready at the same time.

1 pound spiral cut pasta
1 pound boneless chicken breast
2 cans condensed cream of mushroom soup
3 - 4 pickled hot cherry peppers (reserve juice)
4 large pickled (vinegar) peppers (reserve juice). Note: if you cannot find these, you can use pepperocini or pickled pepper rings.
You should have about 1 to 1 1/2 cups combined reserved juice. Keep the hot juice separate from the regular juice. You can adjust to taste.
1/2 teaspoon each salt and pepper
1 tablespoon olive oil (or other oil) enough to coat bottom of your skillet.

1. Put salted pasta water on stove and bring to boil
2. Meanwhile, cut chicken into 1" or so cubes
3. Cut peppers into bite size chunks, removing any excess seeds. (remember to reserve juice)
4. In large skillet add olive and heat. Add cut up chicken and cook until opaque, stirring occasionally.
5. Add peppers, stir. Add 1 can of soup and 1/2 cup regular juice. Stir and lower heat.
6. Add 2nd can of soup and stir. Now taste and adjust tartness by adding either hot juice or more of the regular. Cover pan and reduce heat to low.
7. Pasta water should be boiling at this point. Add pasta to water and cook 7 - 9 minutes, or according to package directions until desired doneness.
8. While pasta is cooking, check on chicken to see if you want to add any more liquid. Turn off heat and keep covered.
9. Drain cooked pasta and pour into large serving dish or bowl.
10. Pour chicken mixture over entire bowl. Stir to blend sauce throughout.

Serve with crusty bread and salad.

Additional note about the peppers: Vinegar peppers are what we always had growing up in an Italian neighborhood. You might know them as pickled peppers. They are the very large peppers sold in jars. Depending of where you are located, you might find these more readily available in stores specializing in Polish, Greek or Italian foods. As mentioned within the recipe, you can use any other kind pickled peppers as a substitute.

Firehouse House Meatloaf

This recipe for Turkey Meatloaf can be adapted using chicken or beef. Like most meatloaf recipes, you can really adjust the seasonings as you wish and still come out with a great tasting dish.

Captain Gene Welischar is a great officer who has a laugh as big as his heart! He is the author of the book, "If You Play With Fire." You will find this recipe referenced there. The firehouse made it for a picnic for the kids at Ronald McDonald House (which was just around the corner from the company quarters). He was Louis's Captain for many years at Engine Co. 22/Ladder Co. 13. His fire house moniker was Mean Gene, The Dancing Machine!

When I first met Gene, I was pretty nervous about meeting Louis's officer. We were at a company function and, as Louis had just gotten on the "job," I wanted to be sure I made a good impression. Captain Welischar and I were introduced and the party went on. Later we saw each other and he addressed me as Gail! I felt uncomfortable correcting him, and never did until many years later. We were at a golf outing that I was running and Gene and several friends were waiting in line to check in with me. His buddies behind him piped in and said, "Who's Gail?" Well, we all laughed and from then on it is one of my favorite stories to tell.

Gene Welischar actually discovered the sauce for this recipe by accident, when sweet potatoes he had added around the baking pan cooked down right into the sauce. Enjoy this recipe from Mean Gene, The Dancing Machine!

The recipe: Firehouse Meatloaf

2 lbs ground turkey
1 1/2 cups flavored Italian breadcrumbs
2 large eggs
1/2 cup mayonnaise
1/2 cup chopped fresh parsley
4 fresh basil leaves chopped
3 cloves finely chopped garlic
1/2 cup grated parmesan or Romano cheese
8 oz. part-skim mozzarella cut into chunks

Sauce:
1 large can tomato sauce
1 large sweet potato, peeled and cooked
1 medium onion, diced
1 glove garlic, chopped

1. Preheat oven to 350
2. Combine all ingredients (except Mozzarella) in a large bowl. Mix gently with hands, careful..don't overwork mixture!
3. Spray 9 x 13 pan with non-stick spray (or coat bottom lightly with oil). Fill pan with meatloaf leaving space around the sides of loaf
4. Randomly place chunks of mozzarella into the loaf, covering them with the meat.
5. Top with sauce.*
6. Bake for 45 minutes to 1 hour.

*Sauce:
1. Mash sweet potato in bowl and add tomato sauce. Stir.
2. Add all other ingredients.
3. Top meatloaf with mixture and bake as above.

Let meatloaf rest for about 10 minutes before you serve. Makes great leftover sandwiches!

Ribs On The Run
Red Wine BBQ Spare Ribs

Life as part of the FDNY family meant that there was always something happening, something always in the works. Planning these events involved lots of teamwork and usually meant putting together mass quantities of food and drink on a budget.

Louis was a great resource when it came to this because he had one of the best "food connections." His cousin, Chris owned a diner, The Polonia, in Manhattan, and he would let us use his vendors to buy all our meats. This was in the days before those food club stores became popular and everyone had access to wholesale buys. Being able to do our shopping in the famous Hunts Point Meat Market was a big deal. Chris knew the best vendors and we always got the best deals. Louis became the go to guy when it came to getting ribs. Ribs, ribs, and more ribs. Ribs, for picnics, ball games, and special parties.

Once the food was purchased the next step was to go about getting it party-ready. It was our job to take care of the ribs. In the world of the spare rib, you have those who like dry seasonings, and those who like wet. No matter what you prefer, the recipe we used then became a must have at all our events. What made it so special? Was it the tangy combination of garlic and soy sauce? Maybe the fact that they were bathing in their marinade for days. Whatever the reason, they remain a favorite to this day.

One of our most memorable rib adventures was getting ready for a "First Grade" party. In the FDNY there were stages you went through once you became a firefighter. During your first year you were on probation (a Proby). The final stage upon which you'd reach the full rank was called First Grade. It was reason to celebrate and celebrate we did! This particular party was for 4 great friends from Engine Co. 22/Ladder Co. 13: Mike Corrigan, Greg "Bro" Stajyk, John Fischer, and Anthony "Don't Call me Tony" Connolly. It would be held at Mike's house out on Long Island. Louis and I were given the rib assignment. Per usual we got the 30 lbs. of ribs and set them to marinating at Chris's restaurant in his walk-in cooler box. The plan was that on the day of the party we would drive to Manhattan, transfer the meat into our cooler and head out to the party. We were about half an hour from Manhattan and then the drive out to Mike's house would take about another hour. No problem — or so we thought!

The morning of the party greeted us with one of the worst rain storms of the season. There were flooded streets and road closings everywhere. We called Mike and learned that the party was still on. Okay, it was now time for us to head down to the Polonia to get the ribs. The rain was coming down in buckets but we made it to the restaurant, packed the ribs into our car and headed east out to Long Island. The highways were flooded and we crawled along at a snail's pace. Throughout the drive the odor of marinating ribs filled the car. What was once a tantalizing aroma became a taunting reminder of our ordeal. We would not give up…we were on a mission to deliver those ribs!

Well, we finally arrived at Mike's where the party was in full swing. It took us a mere 5 hours but we made it! The ribs were none the worse for wear and were soon sizzling on the grill. The rain had let up and was now just an annoying drizzle. It was safe to say that a great time was had by all. The men went on to have full careers in the FDNY. John and Bro made the ultimate sacrifice on 9/11. The spare ribs, the picnics, the parties, the memories. Special times, special friends. Never to be forgotten. Always to be cherished.

The recipe: Ribs on The Run

4 lbs spare ribs (baby back or whatever kind you prefer)
2 cups low-sodium soy sauce
1 cup red wine (use one that you would drink, remember, good stuff in means good stuff out)
1/4 cup sugar
2 tablespoons garlic powder

1. Rinse and pat dry ribs.
2. Place meat in large container with enough space to hold ribs and marinade.
3. Combine soy sauce, wine, sugar, garlic powder in bowl. Stir well.
4. Pour mixture over ribs.
5. Marinate meat for minimum of 1 hour. (We usually do ours for a minimum of 24 hours. If you do marinate them for a long time, you might want to drop in a small, peeled potato to counter the saltiness of the soy.)
6. Heat your grill and start cooking the ribs over medium to low heat for 1 to 1 1/2 hours. Reserve the marinade and brush the ribs while you are cooking them. (When finished, discard any leftover marinade, as you will not be able to use it uncooked). Turn the racks as you cook until done.

Sidor's Fire Starter Peppers
Fried Peppers With Garlic And Anchovies

There are a lot of great hot dishes out there; main courses, appetizers, everything from chicken wings to hot chocolate. This spicy dish is a favorite of mine and a creation of Tom Sidor, retired firefighter from Ladder Company 38, in The Bronx. Tom was a veteran firefighter when my husband, Louis, was assigned to his house as Lieutenant. Tom became his chauffeur, responsible for driving the fire truck to all calls. His expert knowledge made his company one of the top responders in the City of New York at the time. It was a nice plus that Tom also enjoyed navigating around the kitchen. Tom is a very energetic guy and is as enthusiastic about making food as he was about fighting fires. His dishes show it. They're always full of flavor and there's always tons to go around!

Louis and I first had this dish one New Year's Eve at Tom and his wife Linda's home in Weekee Wachee, Florida. We'd recently moved down to the sunshine state from New York and it was one of our first holidays there. Tom's mixture of hot peppers, olive oil, garlic and anchovies makes a great appetizer served with crusty Italian bread. He likes tempting fate with the heat though, and once made a version using all habaneros. Ouch!!!

The recipe is great because you can use any fresh peppers you can find and make it as hot or sweet as you like. It's the combination of ingredients that really makes the dish pop. We like ours hot. It stays in the frig for days and I've used leftovers in scrambled eggs and even over pasta.

The Recipe: Firehouse Peppers with Anchovies

4 Serrano peppers
10 Italian cubanelle peppers
1 can anchovies with capers
6 cloves garlic
3 tablespoons olive oil (you may need more if you prefer a looser dish)

1. Prepare peppers — cut off tops and slice into 1/2's lengthwise. Remove seeds. Slice 1/2 lengthwise again.
2. Coarsely chop garlic cloves.
3. Remove anchovies from can and drain oil. Reserve about 1 teaspoon.
4. Heat olive oil in large skillet until just hot.
5. Add peppers and sauté until softened. If you want them browned a bit, raise your heat until the peppers begin to caramelize. Remove the peppers from the pan and lower the heat.
6. When oil has cooled slightly, add the coarsely chopped garlic. Stir until garlic begins to turn opaque. Be careful not to burn the garlic as it will become bitter.

7. With the heat lowered, add anchovies and stir, combining the garlic, capers and anchovies. The anchovies will breakdown and they will provide the salt for your dish.
8. Raise heat to high and immediately add the peppers back into the pan. Add the reserved anchovy oil and stir. Add any extra olive oil if you find mixture too dry. You may also add salt or pepper if you wish. Stir for a few minutes and then turn off heat.
9. Cover pan and let sit for about an hour before serving. (Keeping the mixture covered will help blend the flavors and infuse the olive oil).

Red Tide Pot Roast
Dennis Mc Donald Special

It is not surprising that so many firehouse dinners echo the comfort meals we had as kids. The Sunday family meal is a rarity in most households these days. Luckily, we can enjoy reading the recipes and, perhaps, become inspired enough to prepare one. Bring back the sit-down dinner every once in a while. It's good for you!

Dennis was a great firefighter who worked with Louis in his very first fire company, Engine Company 22 on 85th Street on the East Side of Manhattan. The firehouse was a double one with both an engine and truck company. Engine 22 and Ladder 13 were known as The Pride of Yorkville. The neighborhood was a lively one filled with a blend of old German restaurants, Irish pubs, "yuppie" bistros. Easy meal shopping was done at Gristedes around the corner on Lexington Avenue.

At the firehouse, everyone had to take their turn at preparing the meal. Louis always called me up to get ideas for his. Coming up with original meals for a large group was a challenge.

Rising to that challenge was Dennis Mc Donald. Dennis was not really known for his culinary arts, but his sense of humor and generous heart well made up for it. An "Old Salt" kind of a guy, the kitchen was not where he chose to spend his spare time; but he always stepped up when called upon, ready for anything. Using a bit of creative (or crazy) license, Dennis took a well-worn Sunday roast recipe and, with the addition of a little tomato sauce among other things, created the legendary Red Tide. Though ominous in name, this delicious dish imparts Dennis's zest for all good things in life. We lost Dennis all too soon but we remember him fondly every time we share old stories and enjoy The Red Tide!

The Recipe: Red Tide Pot Roast
Best prepared in large Dutch Oven

1 3lb roast (eye round, or other meat suitable for slow cooking — if using chuck roast, cut off any excess fat)
3 22oz cans crushed tomatoes
1/2 cup all purpose flour
1 tablespoon salt
1 tablespoon black pepper
1 tablespoon garlic powder
2 stalks celery (cut off top and reserve leaves)
4 carrots
4 medium potatoes (I prefer Yukon Gold for this)
1 large sweet onion
1 package dried French Onion Soup mix

3 tablespoons olive oil
1/4 cup red wine for deglazing pan (you can substitute red wine vinegar or plain water)
1/4 cup water
Salt and Pepper for adjusting seasoning

1. Mix flour, salt, pepper, and garlic in shallow dish for dredging the meat.
2. Finely chop celery leaves and add them the flour mixture (be sure the leaves are dry; you can put them in the microwave wrapped in paper towel for about 30 seconds).
3. Prepare vegetables: Peel, wash, and pat dry potatoes. Wash and pat dry celery stalks and carrots (you can peel the carrots if you wish). Cut potatoes into quarters. Cut carrots and celery into 1" pieces. Peel the onion. Cut in 1/2, then slice in large pieces about 1/2".
4. Open the cans of tomatoes and set aside.
5. Prepare Dutch Oven: add the olive oil and turn heat on to low.
6. Dredge meat completely on all sides in the flour. Pat off any excess but be sure to get all the meat coated.
7. Raise heat to high and place meat in the pot. It should start searing immediately. Reduce heat to medium. Turn meat and let sear a minute or two on all sides until meat is completely seared. Using tongs remove from pot. (Using a fork to remove meat will break the sear. It's also safer to use the tongs.)
8. With heat still on high deglaze pot by adding the red wine. Using a spatula, scrape up all the darkened bits from the bottom. The wine should be cooking down rapidly. Add the additional 1/4 cup water (if needed) to thoroughly deglaze. Reduce heat to low.
9. Add the onion and celery. Stir.
10. Put meat back in pot. Add the canned tomatoes. Use a spatula to stir around meat, making sure that the tomatoes are covering most of the meat (the top may be exposed but that is okay). CAUTION - when you are adding in the tomatoes, they have a tendency to splatter right away. That is why I lower the heat before adding them. I stir as soon as possible after adding each can. This helps control any splattering.
11. Cover the pot and let simmer on medium to low heat for 2 hours. If you are using an electric stove (like me) check every once in a while to ensure that bottom is not burning or sticking. If any sticking does occur, scrape it up and it will get incorporated into the sauce.
12. After about 2 hours your kitchen should smell wonderful. Now add the dried onion soup mix. Stir and continue cooking for 1 hour. Taste and adjust seasonings as you prefer.
13. Add carrots and potatoes. You may want to add more liquid if needed. You can add water, broth, or a little wine. It's up to your taste.
14. Cover and simmer on medium for another 1/2 hour or until potatoes and carrots are cooked through. We like to have our vegetables retain some firmness, which is why I add them last.
15. Turn off heat and let everything sit for about 15 minutes. Remove meat from pot. Again... let it sit while you remove vegetables.
16. Remove all vegetables from the pot and place in a serving dish. Take the pot "gravy" and put in bowl for serving at the table. (Be sure to leave some extra for the meat.)
17. Slice meat to desired thickness and arrange on platter. Spoon gravy over meat. Ready to serve.

Note: This is a great dish to prepare for a party. You can get everything in the pot and then do other party prep while the roast is cooking. If you want a denser sauce (or gravy), remove lid from pot and raise heat. This will cook down excess liquid.

Tasmanian Chicken
Recipe Page: 65

Section III Friends

When I was a Campfire Girl there was a song we used to sing as a troop. It went like this:

"Make new friends but keep the old
One is silver and the other is gold."

How very true that is. Our lifetimes take us down so many varied paths, having a true friend to lean on can mean everything at times.

The kind of neighborhood I grew up in is pretty rare today, especially within large urban areas like New York. I spent all of my childhood and most of my adulthood there. We moved on to other places for a bit, but we were always secure in the fact that our family and friends would be be around when our paths lead us back. We took a big leap when our daughter was very young and left the city altogether to live "semi" off the land in Massachusetts. As Antoinette approached school age, we knew we had to move back to give her access to the best schools.

And so we did. Antoinette, as did Louis and I, went to New York City public schools and flourished. She chose to attend college in the city as well. Louis made a career serving the people of the city as a firefighter, retiring as a Captain; and I made a career with a company that managed most of New York City's public golf facilities. All during this time we lived in Throgg's Neck - blocks from my mom and dad, Louis's mom, cousins, and friends.

Although we have been long gone from the city, having permanently relocated to Florida's Gulf Coast (following our daughter and her family); many of our family and friends remain. We can still go up and visit, walk in to a local restaurant and be greeted warmly with smiles and lots of memories. Yes, the neighborhood has changed, evolving with the times, mirroring the makeup of the city. That only makes it better…new roots taking their place bringing new life.

We move and make new friends; we are bound through love with our old; and with time, the new become old; thus all become golden. Our friends are our treasures. They bring smiles to our faces and tears to our eyes. We hold them close. They help us to carry on.

Recipes in this section:

Pizza Rustica
Cheese Straws
Antoinette's Birthday Meatloaf with Mango Sauce
Linda's Tex-Mex Chicken Casserole
Baked Fish Fillet in a Pouch
Papaya Salsa
Terry's Puerto Rican Style Cooked Beans
Stir Fried Tofu and Watercress
Rugulagh (butter/cream cheese cookies)
Honey Balls

Pizza Rustica

When we moved down to Florida it was a very big step. We sold our home and took the plunge. Louis had just retired from the Fire Department, our second grandchild was about to turn 2. It was time. Luckily it was a pretty seamless adjustment. One of the first things we did was to join a gym, which proved to be a great way to meet people. I took a part-time job there working at the Kid's Club, which turned out to be even better. I got to watch some awesome children grow up and became friends with many of the moms and dads.

One of my best friends was Gina. A young mom, she had 3 kids at the time. We would chat as she dropped off or picked up. It turned out that Gina was from New York (Long Island) and Italian. Ah, common ground. Of course we started talking about food and where to shop for this or that locally. Pizza Rustica came up in a conversation about holiday treats. Pizza Rustica is usually made for Easter. It is a savory custard pie made with cured meats and cheeses. It is rich and a little goes a long way.

Gina is now a mama of 4 beautiful children. We still go to the gym and still can't stop talking about food!

Pizza Rustica: The Recipe

2 deep dish frozen pie shells (at room temperature)
2 links sweet Italian pork sausages
1/2" chunk Mortadella (Italian bologna) cut into small cubes
1/2" chunk Pancetta (Italian bacon) cubed
1 1/2 lb ricotta cheese
1/3 cup grated parmesan cheese
1/4 lb mozzarella cheese
3 large egg yolks
2 leaves basil
1/2 teaspoon salt
1 egg white

1. Cook sausage links in pan. I wouldn't grill them because the grilling flavor would be too strong with this dish. Allow to cool and then cut into cubes.
2. In a large bowl combine the cheeses and egg yolks. Stir with fork to blend.
3. Add in the meats and stir in basil and salt. (You don't need to add pepper because there is pepper in the pancetta.)
4. Take one pie shell and fill with the meat and cheese mixture.
5. Gently take the 2nd shell and layer it over the top of the first one to cover the pie. Seal the edges and cut off any excess.
6. Whisk the egg white and brush over the top the pie.
7. Bake for 1 hour. Allow to cool at least 15 minutes before serving.

Mortadella is sort of an Italian version of bologna. You will find it and pancetta at the deli counter of your supermarket. Just ask the counter person to cut it in one chunk, rather than slicing. Using bologna as a substitute for the mortadella would not work in this recipe because of the spices. Have the pancetta cut the same way.

This is usually an Easter Pie, but make it anytime. What's nice about this pie is that you get little chunks of meat along with the soft custard filling. The natural sweetness of the ricotta and mozzarella counter balance the saltiness of the other ingredients. If you never tried, you are in for a treat,. I like to serve a light marinara sauce on the side, kind of like you would with whipped cream on a sweet pie..

Cheese Straws

These savory snacks were always popping up at parties here in the south. Some were store bought (not bad), some home made (some good, some bad). Our friend, Sue, from the gym, made the best version by far. There's a bit of the true south in every bite. You will get about 40 cheese straws with this recipe.

Spicy Cheese Straws: The Recipe

2 cups grated cheese (half cheddar, half parmesan)
1 tablespoon hot chili powder
1 teaspoon garlic salt
1 package (17 1/2 oz) puff pastry sheets (thawed)
1 egg (beaten)
flour (for work surface)

1. Preheat oven to 400
2. In a medium sized bowl, mix cheese, chili powder, and garlic salt. Set aside.
3. On a lightly floured work surface, roll out 1 pastry sheet into a 15" x 10" rectangle.
4. Brush lightly with the egg.
5. Sprinkle with 1/2 cup cheese mixture. Gently press the cheese into the pastry using a rolling pin.
6. Turn the sheet over and repeat the process with he cheese mixture, again, pressing it into the pastry with a rolling pin.
7. Starting at a 10" end, fold 1/3 of the pastry over the middle 3rd. Fold the opposite 1/3 over both to make a 10" x 5" rectangle.
8. Cut rectangle in half crossways into two 5" squares. Cut each square into 10 1/2" wide strips for a total of 20 pieces.
9. Place strips onto ungreased baking sheets, twisting a few times and pressing ends onto the sheets. This prevents the strips from curling up.
10. Bake for 12 - 15 minutes, or until puffed and golden.
11. Remove straws to wire rack to cool completely.

Store in an air-tight container.

Note: You may have to bake this recipe in 2 batches, depending on how much space you have on your baking sheets, and, of course, on how many sheets you have.

Going Global: Take a side trip to Asia and Mexico with these recipes.

Antoinette's Birthday Chicken Meatloaf

Some recipes become favorites overnight. This is one of them. When our daughter was turning 40 we wanted to throw her a big party. I asked her what she wanted, this was a special time and I wanted to make sure it would be special for her. She asked if I would do a Mexican themed day. She never told me but she had always wanted to have a Piñata party. Well, better late than never, Piñata party it wold be!

It turned out to be a great party, with lots of her friends from near and far helping celebrate. It was a beautiful Florida day and we all whacked at that piñata! I prepared a Mexican/Latin buffet for everyone. The challenge was to come up with dishes that would taste good hot out of the oven and at room temperature too. There were lots of good ones, but this meatloaf dish was a surprise favorite.

I am so happy to say that one of Antoinette's friends (actually the best man at her wedding) took the recipe back home with them. His wife made it for her family and they loved it. It has become their family tradition to serve on special occasions! What an honor.

Antoinette's Birthday Chicken Meatloaf: The Recipe

2 lbs ground chicken (do not use ground breast - it is too lean for this recipe)
1/4 cup fresh cilantro - chopped
1 tablespoon adobo seasoning (found in your International food aisle; if you can't find it or don't have it, substitute with 1 teaspoon garlic powder, 1/2 teaspoon pepper, 1 teaspoon salt)
3 tablespoons ranch dressing (plus 1/4 cup for coating)
1 egg
1/4 cup Italian breadcrumbs plus 2 tablespoons for top, if desired

1. Preheat oven to 350
2. Combine all ingredients in mixing bowl. If too loose, add a bit more breadcrumbs. If to dry, add a bit more dressing.
3. Spray bottom of shallow baking dish with cooking spray. I use a 9" x 13" glass dish for this.
4. Take the meat mixture and form into a loaf. (Ground chicken can get a bit sticky to work with. Wet your hands and this will make it easier.)
5. Transfer formed loaf into the baking dish.
6. Using a pastry brush, coat entire surface and sides of loaf with the ranch dressing.
7. If using breadcrumbs, sprinkle top of coated loaf with them.
8. Bake for about 1/2 hour at 350. Raise heat to 400 and bake 10 more minutes to brown top.

You can prepare this dish in such a short time and it tastes great even after a few days in the frig.

Check out there recipe that follows for a great accompaniment to this meatloaf

Mango Coulis
This recipe may not be as smooth as a traditional coulis, it's kind of like a coulis/salsa hybrid!

What better way to serve the Birthday Meatloaf than with a bit of mango coulis on the side. That's how I served it at Antoinette's party, and how her friends serve it today. You will also find that this recipe is easy to make. It goes great with pork, chicken, and shrimp.

Mango Coulis: The Recipe

2 ripe mangos
1/4 cup fresh cilantro
1 large clove garlic (peeled)
1 teaspoon honey
juice of 1 lime
1/2 teaspoon chili powder (or dried red pepper flakes)
1/2 teaspoon salt

1. Prepare mangos: cut one side of mango, getting your knife just up to the center seed. Slice this piece off. Do the same on the other side of the seed. Remove pulp from the mango skin and cut into chunks.
2. Take the cilantro and coarsely chop.
3. Prepare to blend ingredients: I use a mini-food processor for this, but a blender will work fine.
4. Add garlic clove, cilantro, salt and chili powder to your blender. Pulse a few times to blend.
5. Add mango, lime juice and honey to the mix. Use your blender on puree setting to blend. If using the mini-processor, blend thoroughly on high. All ingredients should be nice and smooth.

That's it! You are now ready to enjoy. You can store this in a sealed container in your frig. It will keep for about a week.

Note on the mangos: when you buy them, make sure they are soft, but not mushy. Too mushy, they may be past their prime and taste off. Too firm and they might be too sour. If your mango is not as sweet as you would like, add a bit more honey to the mix.

Linda's Baked Chicken In Salsa

A dear friend from The Bronx came up with this tasty dish. Linda was the wife of my husband's best friend. We had some great times together. We all loved the Yankees and went to dozens of baseball games. We spent a lot of time visiting each other's homes. Antoinette was a part of this group from the start. In fact, our friend's mom was her first grade teacher! That's the kind of neighborhood it was.

The great thing about Linda was that she loved to cook. She and I would go to restaurants and mentally take apart the recipes, figuring out all their ingredients. We'd go home and cook them up.

There was a quaint restaurant up in Westchester County right along the Bronx River called La Cantina. We use to go there often, Tex-Mex was a new comer to our area at the time and we loved it. Linda and I took the flavors of the chicken chimichanga and fooled around with it. Here's Linda's version. No frying, all fresh ingredients and lots and lots of great flavors.

Linda's Baked Chicken In Salsa: The Recipe

2 lbs boneless chicken breast cut into chunks about 1" or so
1/2 cup adobo seasoning
4 red tomatoes chopped
1 red onion peeled and chopped
1 bell pepper (any color) seeded and chopped
2 avocados (ripe but not too soft) cut into chunks
2 cloves garlic chopped
juice of 1 lime
1 teaspoon salt
1 teaspoon pepper
1 bunch fresh cilantro chopped
1 large bag (16 oz) shredded Monterey Jack cheese (or whatever you prefer, just make sure it melts well)
Olive oil for searing off the chicken

1. Make the salsa - In a bowl gently mix together the chopped vegetables (not the avocado), garlic, cilantro, salt, pepper, and lime juice. Let this sit while you prepare the chicken. If you like a bit of heat, add chopped galleon pepper to the salsa.
2. Dredge the chicken in the adobo, getting each piece coated.
3. In skillet on stovetop add enough olive oil to sear the chicken, but not fry them.
4. When the skillet is hot, add the chicken, searing them just to the point they turn white. Turn them making sure you sear all sides. You don't want to cook them through fully. Just get a little color on them and flavor. Do not over crowd your pan. Do this in batches until all chicken is done.

5. Line an oblong baking dish with the seared chicken pieces.
6. Completely top the chicken with all the salsa.
7. Spread the chunks of avocado over the salsa layer.
8. Spread shredded cheese over all.
9. Bake at 375 for 1/2 hour.
10. Raise heat to 450 and bake an additional 5 minutes or so to brown (not burn!) the cheese.

Linda and I both worked full time and this recipe is a simple, quick, but delicious meal. There is not much clean up and everyone loves it. It goes great with a nice salad and some cooked beans. See the next recipe for Terry's Beans, Puerto Rican Style.

Terry's Puerto Rican Style Beans

I met Terry when I was working at Albert Einstein College of Medicine in The Bronx. Mine was a temporary job giving her a hand organizing patient files for one of the clinics. We clicked right away and are still friends today.

What was great about working at Albert Einstein was that you got to meet people from all walks of life and all different backgrounds and ethnic groups. It was a Jewish hospital and the kitchen where staff ate kept Kosher. That meant that there were days when they served only dairy and days when they served only meat. I hadn't experienced that situation before, and didn't think anything of carrying in lunch from my home (a cup of yogurt). I moved through the food line, along with my friends, getting my beverage. We all sat down at a nearby table and got ready to eat. I was stunned when the man who oversaw the kitchen came running over to us! He took my tray and silverware from me and shouted that he would have to throw everything away! I had contaminated the meat service with my dairy (yogurt)! I was horrified! You can bet that never happened again.

Anyway, in our clinic we had a great mix of staff members. Jewish, Italian (me), African-American, and Puerto Rican. It made for some great office parties. Terry was famous for making rice and beans. I didn't realize how good they could be until I had hers. I make them all the time. You can make one-dish dinners of rice, chicken and beans (arroz con pollo y gandoules); but if you are looking for a very quick and different side dish for dinner, always keep a few cans of good beans in your pantry and whip this up.

Terry's Puerto Rican-Style Beans
Any kind of bean will do, except for black-eyed peas. Pintos, black beans, and kidney beans work great. My favorite is Pigeon Peas. You can also use dried beans, but the canned beans are just fine as long as you rinse them beforehand.

2 cans Pigeon Peas (or your preference)
2 cloves garlic chopped
1 tablespoon fresh cilantro chopped
2 tablespoons green olives with pimento chopped (You can also by jarred olive salad in the pickle aisle or international food aisle. They are already chopped up.)
1 small red onion chopped
1 small bell pepper seeded and chopped
3 tablespoons olive oil
1 teaspoon salt
1 bay leaf

1. Open the beans and place in a colander. Rinse thoroughly under cold water.
2. Take a 3 quart saucepan or dutch oven and add olive oil to the bottom.

3. Heat the oil and add (in this order) onions, bay leaf, bell pepper. Stir and reduce the heat to medium.
4. Add garlic and the olives. Stir.
5. Add the beans and cilantro, stir. Add a bit of water or broth just so they don't stick to your pan.
6. Cover and reduce heat to low.

Beans will be done in about 10 minutes, but the longer they sit, the more flavor they take in. I don't add too much salt to this because of the olives. Beans do need salt, so taste before serving. If need be, adjust the seasoning by adding salt a little at a time.

Baked Fillet in a Pouch

This is my take on foods baked "en papiote" (in paper)

I am always looking for quick and easy ways to make seafood. We have lots of friends who are shying away from red meats and we love all kinds of seafood. We have a restaurant here in Tampa that makes a wonderful pompano en papiote. I use Sea Bass or Salmon, which are easier to come by. Instead of parchment paper, I wrap the fish in foil. Doing this, you can bake the fish indoors, or outside on the grill.

Baked Fillet in a Pouch: The Recipe

4 pieces of firm fish fillet about 4 - 5 oz each (Sea Bass, Salmon, Mahi Mahi)
4 cloves garlic
2 stalks celery and their leaves (chopped)
salt and pepper
1 lemon (sliced)
4 teaspoons olive oil (more it needed)
Aluminum Foil

1. Peel the garlic and cut each one in half lengthwise.
2. Cut the celery stalks into 8 pieces. Make sure to save any leaves.
3. Take each fillet and rub with olive oil.
4. Cut 4 pieces of foil large enough to hold your fish, allowing for folding, kind of like wrapping a gift. Probably about 1 1/2 times your fish size.
5. Spray foil with cooking spray or lightly brush with oil to prevent sticking.
6. Cut celery stalks into 3" sections. They will act as the rack for your fish. Cut enough for the amount of fillets you are baking You'll need 2 to 3 each depending on the fillet size.
7. Place fish in center of foil on top of the celery.
8. Sprinkle top of fish with salt and pepper.
9. Place slices of lemon over top of fish.
10. Place 2 pieces of garlic on top of the lemon.
11. Place the celery leaves along the top of the fish.
12. Take foil from 2 opposite sides and fold together tightly closing on top of the fish. Leave room above the fish for steaming, about 1/2".
13. Fold over the other 2 sides of foil kind of rolling them over each other making little handles on each side.
14. Place in preheated 375 oven and cook until done. For Sea Bass, about 20 minutes, salmon - about 15, mahi mahi - about 20.

When you remove the fish from the oven, let stand a few minutes to allow for the flavors to set in. As you open the pouches, you will smell the aroma of the celery and lemon all intermingled with the garlic and the seafood.

This goes great with papaya salsa. That recipe is next.

Papaya Salsa

My mom loved trying all kinds of different foods. In our neighborhood, though, we only had Italian or Chinese restaurants and the closest thing we had to a gourmet shop was the deli up the "block." My mom and dad loved searching out fun foods to try and my first taste of so-called Mexican food was a can of tamales. Canned tamales are not as bad as they sound and I really loved the spicy red sauce. Needless to say times changed and Southwestern Mexican food became part of the American diet. Nachos and salsa are even served in movie theaters.

Having moved to Florida, we were delighted to find wonderful tropical fruits and vegetables available all year round. Finding papayas and mangos readily at the vegetable stand in mid-winter was fantastic. I could make salsa from these whenever I wanted!

Papaya is a really great fruit. Making salsa from papaya is a nice change from the usual. It goes great with seafood and lighter meats. Try thinking outside the jarred salsa box and check out what your local fruit and vegetable stand has on hand. Use your imagination, there's really no wrong way to go.

1 medium papaya
2 green jalapeño peppers
1 small red onion chopped
1 tablespoon cilantro chopped
1 fresh lime and zest
1 clove garlic finely chopped
Salt and pepper to taste (about 1/2 teaspoon each)
1/2 teaspoon honey

1. Prepare the papaya: Cut in half lengthwise and remove all the black seeds. Remove the opaque inner membrane from the center cavity. Peel each half and then quarter it. dice and place in a mixing bowl.
2. Peppers: Slice and seed the peppers, Remove the membrane as well. Slice into strips and then dice into small pieces. Place in the bowl with the papaya.
3. Add the onion and cilantro.
4. Using a plane or zester, grate the outer lime zest into the bowl.
5. Juice the lime (if it is very hard, put it in the microwave for 20 seconds, that will help get the juices out). Add the lime juice to the bowl.
6. Add honey and salt and pepper.
7. Gently fold the mixture taking care not to pulverize the fruit.
8. Pour into a storage bowl and refrigerate until ready to serve.

This is an easy dish that can be served as an appetizer of condiment. Try it, you'll impress your friends. Note: this recipe works well using peaches too.

Stir Fried Tofu and Watercress

We love Chinese food and Asian flavors. I went to high school in Manhattan and had a lot of Asian friends. We used to go down to Chinatown and they would guide me through the grocery store, introducing me to yummy snacks like dried plum with salt, cuttlefish, and shrimp chips.

One of our friends through the Fire Department was retired Battalion Chief Bartly Mitchell. Bart's wife, Nancy was Chinese. Coincidentally she grew up just a few blocks away from Louis in Harlem. One of our best times was getting together with the Mitchell's for a farewell dinner before we moved to Florida. There was a great Chinese restaurant in Yonkers that Nancy and Bart loved and they took us there. No menus needed here. Nancy had the waters bring us all different courses of all varieties of foods. Not the usual fare, local "insider stuff." It was truly a night to remember.

This is yet, another very simple dish taking just minutes to make but it is great. You can have it alone as a light lunch, or as a side dish with your main meal.

Stir Fried Tofu and Watercress: The Recipe

1 bag watercress
1 block extra firm tofu
1 tablespoon hot chili sauce (Sriracha is readily available in most stores)
1 teaspoon soy sauce
2 cloves garlic chopped
1/2 teaspoon sesame oil
2 tablespoons vegetable oil
2 scallions (green parts only) chopped

1. Prepare your watercress by chopping it so that it is easy to stir in the wok or skillet. I usually rough cut the stems into about 2" pieces.
2. Prepare the tofu: Remove from package and drain the water. Take a paper towel and wrap completely around the tofu, pressing to extract the water. Discard the wet towel and wrap again in new one. Set block in a shallow bowl and place a heavy plate on top to help get rid of the excess water. Let that sit bout 5 minutes.
3. Cut the tofu into 1/2" cubes.
4. Heat your wok or skillet, add 1 tablespoon oil.
5. Quickly toss in the tofu and add the oil, soy sauce, sesame oil and garlic.
6. Toss tofu to get the flavors mixed in.
7. Add the chili sauce.
8. Add the watercress and remove from heat.
9. Toss the tofu/watercress just to the point where the cress has wilted.
10. Transfer to serving bowl and garnish with the chopped scallions.

Summer or Spring Rolls

I was introduced to these rolls by another Chinese friend. She lived just off the Grand Concourse in the Bronx and I would often take the bus over to visit. The Grand Concourse was predominantly Jewish at that time. Who would guess that there was a great Chinese restaurant tucked away just east of 170th Street? Just as with Nancy, it was great going into these restaurants with someone who knew the language. We always got special treatment and, according to them, always go the very best fortunes.

Summer or Spring Rolls: The Recipe

Summer are made just by dipping the rice wrappers in cold water and wrapping ingredients in them.
Spring are doing the same as above but frying them after wrapping.

For both you will need:
1 package round rice papers
thin sliced ingredients for the filling
large flat dish (I use pie plate) for the water
smooth, dry surface for wrapping

Vegetable summer rolls:
1 cucumber (peeled and cut lengthwise, then seeded and patted dry)
1 small head savoy cabbage (chop off heel and rinse leaves, then pat dry)
1 bunch cilantro (or flat leaf parsley if preferred) washed and patted dry. Mint can work too.
3 carrots (peeled and pat dry)
1 bunch scallions (rinsed, dried, stub ends chopped off)
1/4 cup Hoison sauce (if you don't have this, then you can use Chinese 5 spice powder)

You may also add for non-veg: chilled, thinly sliced cooked shrimp or chicken breast

Prep veggies as follows:
1. Cucumber: take the 2 lengthwise pieces and cut in half. Then cut each half into about 1/4" thick spears
2. Cabbage: Take bunch of leaves and cut into about 6" long pieces. Where needed, cut out hard rib. These will give depth to the roll. If you don't like the cabbage, you can use bib lettuce.
3. Carrots: Cut carrots into 6" lengths. Taking a vegetable peeler, peel thick slices of carrot lengthwise.
4. Cilantro: Trim excess lengths of stem from bunch. You want to keep them leafy and about same length as other veggies but you can fold them as well.
5. Scallions: These should be cut into smaller lengths, maybe about 2" each. Otherwise when you bite into the roll they will come out as a whole!

Get ready to roll:

1. Fill dipping bowl with enough water so that you can completely cover rice paper.
2. Have your veggies and Hoison Sauce assembled next to the dry area where you will place your dipped paper. You will need a brush or teaspoon for the sauce.
3. Take 1 sheet of paper and dip into the bowl. Tapping lightly with your fingers, make sure it is completely covered. Now carefully lift sheet out of bowl. Kind of hang it so that it smooths out.
4. Lay flat on surface and add: cucumber, cabbage, scallion, carrots, protein (if you want) then cilantro. Brush filling lightly with Hoison sauce (or drop lightly). If using powder, sprinkle lightly over filing. These should be in the center of the paper about and inch down from the top.
5. Gently take top of paper and bring forward over filling. Now take one side and fold inward. Then take next side and fold inward. Continue rolling paper until all wrapper. Set aside on platter, seam side down, covered with wax paper (so rolls won't stick).

Continue until you have the amount of rolls you want. Add more water to dipping bowl as needed. Save any unused rice papers for next use. Store in zip lock bag in cupboard or frig.

Serve chilled rolls with sweet red chili sauce.

Rugelach - Rolled Cream Cheese Cookies

Rugelach (pronounced Roo-ga-lah) are filled cookies, baked with a cream cheese and butter dough. They are a traditional Jewish pastry that are eaten all through the year.

How I Met My Jewish Mothers: Louis and I had been living outside New York City for a few years. Our daughter, Antoinette, was approaching school age and we knew it was time for us to head home. Albert Einstein College of Medicine (AECOM) is a huge hospital/university complex in the Pelham Bay section of The Bronx, not far from Throgg's Neck where we lived.

Purely by chance, both Louis and I were able to get jobs there. Louis's was at one facility and mine was in another. These jobs turned out to be major stepping stones for us, enabling us to start building a financial base and giving Louis the time to study and pass the exam for the fire department.

My position at AECOM was a temporary one, as were many at the college, funded through any number of specific grants. When the grant money ran out, the job did too. My job was a low-level clerical one, but in a specialized clinic. The staff at the clinic were from all different backgrounds, but everyone worked together so well. It really was like a big family - a little drama, a lot of good times. From my very first day I began hoping that the grant money would be extended and my position would as well.

My boss then was a wonderful woman named Estelle. Estelle's assistant was Miriam. These two ladies took me under their wing and taught me so much. Two typical "Jewish mothers," they made sure I had everything I needed to be a success.

Estelle fought for the grant money to be extended. She was able to use these funds to transition my position to a permanent one (and provide for my promotion to an administrative one). I remained at Albert Einstein for seven years. Thanks to Estelle's belief in me and the tuition reimbursement plan at AECOM, I was able to complete NYU's Diploma Course in Computer Technology.

Sadly, Miriam passed away suddenly during that time, but Estelle (now in her late 80's) and I remain friends to this day. These Rugelach cookies were a favorite of Miriam's.

Rugelach: The Recipe

2 cups flour
1/2 teaspoon salt
1 cup unsalted butter (chilled)
1 8oz package of cream cheese (chilled)
1/3 cup sour cream
1/2 cup white sugar

1 tablespoon cinnamon
1 cup finely chopped walnuts
1/2 cup raisins
2 tablespoons sugar (for topping)
1 teaspoon cinnamon (for topping)

1. Cut the chilled butter and cream cheese into small cubes. In food processor pulse flour, salt, butter, cream cheese and sour cream until crumbly. If you don't have a food processor, use a fork and mix until you get the same result.
2. Shape the crumbly mixture into four balls. Wrap each ball in wax paper or plastic wrap and chill for 2 hours.
3. Combine your filling mixture: cinnamon, walnuts, raisins.*
4. Remove dough (one at at time) from refrigerator and roll each into about a 9" round. You want to only take out the one you're working on. The dough works best when cold.
5. Sprinkle each round with the filling mixture. Press lightly into the dough.
6. Cut each round into 12 wedges. Roll wedges from wide end to narrow ending with he pointed tip on the outside of the cookie.
7. Combine the topping sugar and cinnamon in small bowl.
8. Sprinkle lightly over cookies. Place on ungreased baking sheet and chill for about 20 minutes before baking.
9. Repeat the process for each ball of dough.
10. Preheat oven to 350.
11. Bake in center rack for 20 - 22 minutes until lightly golden. Set to cool on wire racks.

*You can substitute small chocolate chips for the raisins. Other fillings you can use are apricot jam, almond paste.

Neopolitan Honey Balls - Struffilo

It seems like wherever you going this world, you will find a version of fried dough. It transcends all economic backgrounds.

My dear friend, Margaret and I have been friends since I was 10. Margaret and I used to gather in her kitchen around Christmastime to make batches of these sticky, sweet and addictive treats. Margaret's mom always hosted Christmas Eve dinner for their family. Having 2 sisters and 1 brother, plus their families - that was one big dinner.

With my husband, Louis, being in the fire department, Christmas Eve and Christmas Day were often work days for him. Anytime this happened, Margaret's mom and dad always welcomed Antoinette and me into their home to join their celebration.

Struffilo are served during both Christmas and Easter.

Neopolian Honoey Balls: The Recipe:

1/2 cup sugar plus 1 teaspoon
3 large eggs
1 tablespoon butter (room temperature0
2 cups flour
1/2 teaspoon baking powder
1 cup honey (you can add 1/2 teaspoon cinnamon if you like)
rainbow sprinkles
Vegetable oil for deep frying
Flour for your surface and to work with the dough

1. In a bowl, whisk together the egg, butter and 1 teaspoon sugar until foamy.
2. Sift the flour with the baking powder and stir into the egg mixture.
3. Using your hands, work the mixture into a soft dough. divide into 4 pieces.
4. On a floured surface, roll each piece into a rope about finger width and 12 inches long.
5. Cut roped into 1" pieces.
6. Toss with just enough flour to dust lightly, shaking off any excess.
7. In a deep fryer or a pot with sides deep enough for frying heat oil to 375 or bubbling.
8. Fry the balls a few handfuls at a time until they are puffed and turn golden brown.
9. Using slotted spoon transfer to platter lined with paper towel to drain.
10. Continue frying all the balls.
11. In a large saucepan, combine the honey and 1/2 cup sugar.
12. Heat over low heat, stirring, until the sugar has dissolved.
13. Keep this mixture over very low heat and add the fried balls a bit at a time, turning them with with wooden spoon to coat.
14. Transfer each batch of coated balls to your serving plate (a deep dish pie plate is great).

15. Mound the struffilo into pyramid as you go.
16. Sprinkle the finished platter with rainbow sprinkles.
17. Let stand for at least 1 hour.

To eat these treats, just break off whatever you want from the pyramid with your hand or a spoon.

Platters of struffilo are often served at weddings. In addition to the rainbow sprinkles, they are adorned with colorful Jordan almonds.

Antoinette's Birthday Chicken Meatloaf
Recipe page: 76

Baked Fillet in a Pouch
Recipe page: 82

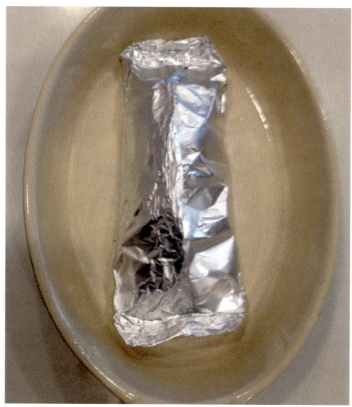

Some notes about this book:

There are a few recipes that call for the use of dried bay leaves. Remember to remove these once you have finished cooking.

Please adapt the seasonings to your individual tastes. Most of these recipes are simply favorites of family and friends and the recipes are based on their tastes.

Some photos of the people and places that helped make this book possible.

**Aunt Ida, her daughter, Terry, and me at Tampa's Hard Rock Casino.
Aunt's Ida's recipe: Ricotta Cake, page 24.**

FDNY City-Wide Softball Champions! Members of Engine Company 22/Ladder Company 13, back in the late 70's. Gene Welischar is pictured second from right rear in the dark sweatshirt. My husband, Louis is bottom row second from left with mustache and ball cap. The team played every Thursday in Central Park and on Randalls Island in Manhattan. Gene Welischar's Recipe: Firehouse Meatloaf page 67.

Tom Sidor with wife Linda, and son Damien in Tarpon Springs, Florida 1999. Tom's recipe: Firestarter Peppers, page 64

My sister Donna (L), me, and my husband Louis.   Donna winning "big" at Saratoga Racetrack, Saratoga, New York
Donna's recipes:
Mashed Potato Pie, page 21
Beauty Shoppe Carrot Cake, page 27

My Dad was in his glory when we visited Castroville, Ca. Pictured below are me, my cousin Walt's two boys, Jim and John, my mother Mary, and my dad, Lou - The Artichoke King!
Lou's Recipes:
Baked Stuffed Artichokes, page 7
Swiss Roll Meatloaf, page 16

Antoinette's 40th Birthday Piñata Party. From Left: Antoinette, (front) grandson Travis, (back) Louis, Me, Grandson Lucas, Son-in-law Jerry.
The recipe: Antoinette's Birthday Chicken Meatloaf, page 76.

My mother-in-law, Eleni learned most of her great recipes during afternoons spent in the park on Riverside Drive, in New York City's upper west side. Eleni would meet up with other young moms, also Greek immigrants, sharing recipes and making long-lasting friendships.
In the photo below are my husband, Louis, his brother John, and Eleni, in Riverside Park.

Following the Turkish invasion of Cyprus, many of Louis's family came to the United States. Here we have (from left to right) Mike and Despina, Loulla, Aunt Melia, Loulla's husband, Steve, me, Louis, and George. This photo was taken in the late 1970's at a family wedding. Mike and Despina had just arrived.

My Grandmother Barbara Kleh, and my Grandfather Joseph F. Testa. This photograph was taken in their first apartment on Villa Avenue in the Bronx.

Photo of Mary and Lou Testa (my mom and dad) in Rochester, New York, while visiting Mary's family shortly after World War II.

My Sister Donna (R) and I playing in our yard on Valentine Avenue, The Bronx.

My mother, me, and Donna at Bronx Park, in the Fordham Section of The Bronx.

Donna and I playing in our backyard "pool." This photo was taken just after we moved to Throgg's Neck. The yard was all dirt and my mom used old cardboard boxes as a liner underneath the pool so that it wouldn't leak.

So here were are today. None the worse for wear. Celebrating Travis's confirmation in Safety Harbor, Florida, May 2016. From left: Louis, Lucas, Travis and me.

Happy Cooking!

Made in the USA
San Bernardino, CA
23 July 2016